COSMIC YEAR

COSMIC YEAR

Your Astrological Guide to Co-Creating with the Planets

Claire Gallagher

SHAMBHALA

Shambhala Publications, Inc.
2129 13th Street
Boulder, Colorado 80302
www.shambhala.com

Cover and interior design: Meredith Jarrett

9 8 7 6 5 4 3 2 1

First Edition
Printed in the United States of America

Shambhala Publications makes every effort to print on acid-free, recycled paper. Shambhala Publications is distributed worldwide by Penguin Random House, Inc., and its subsidiaries.

Library of Congress Cataloging-in-Publication Data
Names: Gallagher, Claire, author.
Title: Cosmic year: your astrological guide to co-creating with the planets / Claire Gallagher.
Description: First edition. | Boulder, Colorado: Shambhala [2026] | Includes bibliographical references.
Identifiers: LCCN 2025051307 | ISBN 9781645474944 trade paperback
Subjects: LCSH: Astrology
Classification: LCC BF1708.1 .G338 2026 | DDC 133.5—dc23/eng/20251231
LC record available at https://lccn.loc.gov/2025051307

The authorized representative in the EU for product safety and compliance is eucomply OÜ, Pärnu mnt 139b-14, 11317 Tallinn, Estonia, hello@eucompliancepartner.com.

To Conor and Tegan. May you find a passion that delights you as much as astrology delights me.

Contents

Contents

Introduction

I found my first Moon journal yesterday. As I flipped through the pages, I was overcome with compassion for my younger self. She was so afraid. She braced for every eclipse as if it were going to ruin her life, and every retrograde threatened a breakup or a health crisis. She manipulated astrology to confirm her suspicion that the sky—and therefore life—was out to get her. Sounds awful, doesn't it?

As I became a professional astrologer, I noticed that I was in good company. At first, I tended to attract clients who were just like me: people who were fascinated by astrology but full of fear. It was like a big mirror had been placed in front of my face, and I was able to see what I was doing with fresh eyes. I was using astrology to magnify my beliefs, and those beliefs needed some adjusting.

When you filter astrology through thoughts like *Nothing works out for me* or *I'll always be miserable,* of course it's going to feel less than supportive. So I struck a deal. If I wanted to keep astrology in my life, I had to change my relationship with it, and I had to address my underlying beliefs with compassion.

I'm hardwired to see what's wrong. I'm a great astrological diagnostician. (You can see it in my birth chart. It's represented by a very tough aspect.) But I also know that when something in the birth chart is tough, it often becomes a personal calling—a thing you're destined to "fix." I began to see my deep fear as fuel for my practice. It became my mission to rebalance my astro-negativity bias and figure out how astrology could be therapeutic not just for my clients but also for myself. So I set out to brainstorm how astrology could help me and my clients take care of *right now*, no matter how joyful or gut-wrenching right now might be.

To do this, I made a weird choice for a professional astrologer: I took a break from the future. I stopped looking ahead in my astrology almanac, restructured my entire practice and stopped offering year-ahead readings, and didn't consume any type of forecast. I knew I had no business looking at the future until I could address what was happening in my body and mind right now with kindness. My focus became *What's the astrology right now? What does it offer? And what would help?*

This break from the future was important. I needed the space, and I highly recommend it if your story is anything like mine. But there came a time when the future whispered, *Hey, we have important work to do*. So from a refreshed place, I opened myself back up to the cycles of time. There were so many powerful techniques (such as the ones in this book) that I missed using. I wanted to explore how I could use them in a way that wasn't fear-based but that also didn't bypass the truth—that life is complex and sometimes it's hard.

Maybe I'm just extraordinarily stubborn, but it tends to take an exaggerated pendulum swing for me to come back to center. After my strict season of no peeking, I was able to make peace with the future and come to terms with the fact that it's just human nature to be curious about it. But there is a skillful way to do it, and the book you're holding is my humble attempt to explore that way.

At the center of astrology is the argument of fate versus free will. I must admit I waver between the two camps depending on how I'm feeling and what's going on. But this book hinges on the belief that you can do something with the energy you've been dealt, even if it hurts. I now believe that, at its core, the Universe and its cycles are benevolent and ultimately have our best interests in mind. That belief gets shaken at times, but it sure beats the alternative.

It might be tempting for you to use this book to wonder or worry about times that aren't here yet. And you certainly could do that. I'm giving you all the tools you need to plot the ups and downs of life. But I don't recommend it. Of course, do what you want, but as someone who's worked in this field for a good bit of time, I rarely see that as therapeutic. Rather, I encourage you to focus on what's here right now instead of what's coming. I believe that taking care of yourself in the present (what these chapters are intended to help you do) is the best way to prepare yourself for the future.

Here I offer a collection of tools, organized by each planet, to help you go inward and feel your way forward. These tools are meant to lead you back to yourself. It's my mission in every sentence to point you back to your inner wisdom. The planets are simply an elaborate (and fun) metaphor to help you do just that.

COSMIC YEAR

one

Not Just a Birthday

It was gloriously hot—just how I like it. The sky was cloudless, and the dock gently rocked back and forth. I had my coffee and my bright, tangerine-colored journal. I felt that familiar swelling of hope in my chest, hope that this year would be different. This would be the year when I finally put a dent in my dreams. It was August 27, 2024, and I had just finished my birthday ritual. I'd reflected on the past year, written down my intentions for the new one, and checked in with my upcoming astrology, being sure to chat with my co-creator planet about what's to come.

I was never a birthday person until I became an astrologer, but now my birthday feels like a high holy day: not because I demand gifts or celebration (although that's always nice), but because the veil between me and the unseen world is thin. This ritual of reflecting, dreaming, and then reading the cosmic weather is a magical time when the fates whisper to me about the future. It's become my favorite moment of the year.

Whether you love them or hate them, birthdays are heavy with meaning. This personal yearly cycle is something we inherently know to be sacred. This cycle, like all cycles, is a returning. It offers you an opportunity to meet yourself fresh. It's about renewal and, ultimately, about hope. It brings second, third, fourth, hundredth chances and a deep knowing that you've been here before, and yes, you can be here again—maybe even with a little more wisdom and compassion this time around. Ideally, cycles are a spiraling upward.

What I love about astrology is that it offers us even more cycles to mark and celebrate. I bet you can name some astrological cycles right now. Mercury retrograde, anyone? That's probably the most popular. Don't forget Venus and Mars retrograde too. Then there's the eclipse cycle, of course, and the ever-famous Saturn return. And although I do address these popularized astrology cycles in this book, the yearly cycle is the one I encourage you to focus on first. Why? Well, each year of your life is overseen by a particular planet. All the planets take turns directing life with you and knowing whose turn it is is invaluable. This handing over of life from planet to planet is a cycle that repeats until you leave this earth. And it happens on your birthday.

Have you ever noticed that each year seems to have its own personality? We tend to say things like "1995 was a great year" or "2021 was the year from hell" or "I haven't been the same since 2005." And then some years just seem to fade into a blur. This has always fascinated me. How can the same old cycle feel so different from one to the next? Thanks to astrology, I have a lot more insight into that now. It has everything to do with that planet—the one that's directing your year.

Time Lords and Co-Creators

In traditional astrology, this planet is called your time lord (best said with a posh accent). Sounds kind of bossy, right? I actually like the phrase *time lord*. It's fun to say, but I think it creates a few problems too. *Time lord* implies that you've been dethroned and that you're no longer in charge of how things go. It creates a power dynamic between you and a planet, putting you at the bottom and the planet at the top. I prefer to take a more empowered approach, so I'm rebranding time lords in this book as *co-creators*.

A co-creator works alongside you. You're a team. You collaborate, share, and make decisions together. You use each other as a resource. One of you may be great at one thing, and one may be great at another—combining your forces equals excellence. As you can imagine, you really want to know who your co-creator planet is so that you can make friends. You want to know its gifts and strengths so that you can leverage them.

I like to imagine my time lord (ahem, co-creator) as an eager assistant or a loyal best friend who can't wait to help me out. I also like to imagine that my co-creator isn't nosy, meaning it doesn't meddle in my affairs unless I ask it to. And, yes, I ask it to. But I give it very clear instructions.

Here's some insight I received from Jupiter when it was my co-creator. I share this personal journal excerpt because I think it really illustrates the *time lord* versus *co-creator* concept. (By the way, I'll teach you how to chat with your co-creator later.)

> Give me permission to act on your behalf and do great things for you. I'm not going to force it. I need your permission and direction. It delights me to work for you. I wish you would let me do it more often. Really. Please boss me around. Give me a daily to-do list and I'll be salivating to do it. Remember, your happiness and success are my top priority.
>
> —JUPITER

Okay, Jupiter! Will do. Your co-creator is just as excited to support you.

Although there are many astrological techniques for identifying your co-creator planet, and I juggle multiple in my professional practice, in this book, I'm presenting one—the one that I find to be the most profound and accessible. It's an ancient timing technique called annual profections, and we'll dive deeply into it soon. But I just want you to know from the outset that, although I couldn't fit it in these pages, there's way more astrology where this came from. Let this book be a springboard for exploring other ancient time-lord techniques if they call to you, such as the minor periods and ascensional times, circumambulations, zodiacal releasing, and more.

Your Birth Chart Is Alive

Before we get started, you might want to have a copy of your birth (natal) chart handy. One with whole-sign houses (where one house corresponds with one entire zodiac sign) is best. If you don't yet have one, check out the "Resources" section in the back of the book for my recommendations on how and where to get one. And, once you have it in hand, if you're unsure what all those symbols on your chart represent, I've included a glyph key in the appendix that shows you the symbols and their corresponding planets and zodiac signs.

As an astrologer, the part about the yearly cycle that I geek out on the most is that it teaches you more about your birth chart than any book or course ever could. Nothing is more eye-opening than a year "turning on" a part of your chart and saying, *Hey, watch this.* When a part of your chart is activated, you get a master class in what that part is all about.

For example, if your co-creator is Jupiter, your natal Jupiter will be turned on, and the house it's located in, the other houses it has influence over, and any aspects it's a part of will become hot. These are the parts of you that you get to explore and develop and the parts of your life that you get to grow.

Here's the thing: Not everything in your birth chart is active all the time. That may be news to you. Sure, if you view astrology as just a personality profile, then parts of your chart will always express through you. But if you view your chart as a map of potential, a map of life events and experiences, then be relieved that it's not all happening at once. Personally, I would implode.

It's like your chart is a home with lots of rooms, and your co-creator planet walks into a certain room and flips on the light switch. Ta-da! Maybe you've spent a lot of time in this room, and it's familiar and comfortable, or maybe it's the cellar that you're a little creeped out by and try to avoid. Like I said earlier, cycles bring you home to a part of yourself—some parts are familiar, and some are foreign.

Presence Before Prediction

In this book, I give you all the tools you need to predict the quality of your year for years to come. However, as I said before, I don't recommend it. But let's be real: Who's really going to listen to that advice? So instead, I suggest practicing presence *before* prediction. Commit to anchoring yourself first before looking ahead. *Presence* is a really loaded word. It's bloated with images of incense and spa music and fountains. It's kind of lost its meaning. Let's flesh it out and give it some substance.

To me, being present means feeling the sensations that are coming up in your body right now, whether they're pleasant or unpleasant. It's a moment of noticing, labeling, and welcoming. For example, right now I'm feeling some pain in my left hip from sitting at my desk for so long. I'm noticing the pressure of my ankles crossing over one another, and I'm noticing that my lips feel dry and rough.

Being present means acknowledging any emotional states without trying to change them. Perhaps you're used to stuffing feelings down or demanding that they shift. Presence doesn't have demands. For example, I'm noticing that I feel some self-judgment and insecurity as I type. An easy thing I like to do is to talk to these feelings. *Hi, self-judgment. Hi, insecurity. You're welcome to sit with me as I write.* To me, being present means being with how you are right now, not forcing yourself to be different.

Being present also means connecting with your immediate surroundings. This is as simple as taking a look around the room you're in and just noticing what's there. It can be helpful to label things and simplify them into colors and shapes: desk, plant, window, lamp, square, rectangle, yellow circle.

But presence isn't completely passive. There's power in it. Once you become present and pause, you can begin to gently adjust. Now that you've gathered the information about your experience, you can begin to create more comfort and ease for yourself. This may feel foreign at first, but one way I like to do this is to simply ask myself a basic question: *Do I need anything?* I like to put a hand on my heart and use a pet name too: *Hey, sweetheart, what can I get you?* Maybe nothing comes up at first, but give your body a chance to answer. As it builds trust with you, it'll begin to talk. If you get an answer, see if you can give that thing to yourself. Follow the guidance.

So when I say presence before prediction, this is all I mean. Take a moment to pause, drop in, and support yourself now before catapulting yourself into the future.

Plus, the thing about the future is that you really don't know the full context. You might be able to make a mirage-like prediction, but you really have no idea about the circumstances or context surrounding that future situation. You're also probably not taking into account how you will change between now and then. You're going to mature. You're going to gather tools and ways of not just coping but thriving. And what you want is most likely going to change too. Who's to say that what you want now is what you'll want then? The best way to prepare for a future cycle is to be with the cycle that's happening right now. If you strengthen your being-with muscle, you can attend to anything that comes up in the future with maturity and compassion.

Prediction as Future-Self Care

After all my harping on being present before predicting, let's talk about the benefits of prediction for a second. Is there any therapeutic value in knowing something may be hard before it happens? This is a really tough question that I ask myself constantly as a consulting astrologer. I'm still coming to peace with this struggle, but here's where I've landed so far.

I have some family members preparing for a mountaineering trip right now. They know the journey is going to challenge them and that it's probably going to push their bodies and minds to the limit. Why is knowing this helpful? One, they can prepare themselves. They can train their legs to climb and their lungs to thrive at high altitudes. They can prepare their minds by understanding the length of the journey, what the plan is, and what obstacles to expect. They can also hire a guide to help them along the way—someone who can support them when things get tough.

It's the same idea when you're looking at the future astrology and notice that something is likely to push you. When you know an upcoming year might be challenging, you can use the capacity you have *now*, the energy and support you have *now*, to prepare for that time. You'll be sure to "pack" the right supplies and strengthen your mindset, knowing that you'll need to be mentally and emotionally resilient. And just like hiring a guide, you may even take the time to get your support system in place.

Another benefit of knowing that something may stretch you is that it becomes less personal when and if it happens. A lot of times we think a difficult situation is our fault and that we must've done something wrong to precipitate a disappointment or a struggle. We think that if we had just worked harder or been "better," it wouldn't have happened. But astrology gives us a new way of thinking about hard times. Cycles come to everyone indiscriminately. When you know that a cycle's quality has nothing to do with your performance or your value or worth, you can just let that pressure go. It's not your fault. Some cycles are objectively and subjectively pleasant; some are less so. It's simply the nature of time.

And finally, if you know something will require effort and endurance, you're less likely to jump ship or abandon yourself when the tough times come. You knew they were coming, and now that they're here, you can sink in, hunker down, and address them in whatever way they need. In this way, foresight fosters even greater presence.

Prediction Pep Talk

As someone who's watched and worked with astrological cycles for many years, I have a few more perspective shifts to offer you. First, I've noticed that "difficult" years (typically those directed by Saturn or Mars) often unfold differently than you expect or in a much subtler way than outright strife. For example, a year that activates a tricky placement in your natal chart may, yes, describe a hard experience you endure, but it may also describe how you turn that experience into a strength. When you have something "weak" or poorly placed in your chart, it might be pointing to a problem that you're here to solve or a group of people that you're here to serve. Keep in mind that challenging placements have the potential to transform into a personal mission or an avenue of service.

If we only experienced "good" cycles, we would never face our inner demons and come out on the other side. We would never have the opportunity to heal. "Difficult" cycles allow us to come face-to-face with what needs our attention and compassion. They offer us a chance to transmute our suffering into a gift for ourselves and others. Without them there would be no triumph.

Second, sometimes "challenging" cycles simply show up as something new that you've never experienced before. These out-of-the-ordinary experiences require you to ask new questions and take new approaches. They're not bad; they're just different. They stretch you beyond your comfort zone, helping you build your confidence long-term.

And third, remember that the sky is always moving and shifting and that any "bad" cycle is only temporary. The word *cycle* itself implies motion and repetition. Each time around you have more experience, more tools, and more proof that you're strong and capable. You have more wisdom and agency.

How to Handle Astrology Fear

I hope I have soothed any fear or hesitation you have by this point, but no matter how many pep talks I give you, it's only human to feel some fear. I don't want to turn you loose into the world of predictive astrology without a tool kit, so let's chat about what to do if and when astrology fear does pop up.

• • • • • • •

Step 1: Pause

First, stop and feel the fear before reaching for a distraction. Put a hand on your heart and notice what's going on in your body. Validate your experience. Tell yourself that it makes sense that you feel this way. Then, if there's something you can do to create a little calm, go ahead and do that. Maybe it's wiggling your toes, taking a few big breaths, or letting out an audible sigh.

Step 2: Talk to It

Create some separation from your astrology fear by recognizing it as just one part of you instead of the whole. Also notice that this part is acting from a place of protection. Instead of stuffing it down, talk to it directly. The conversation may go something like this:

Hey, astro fear. I see and hear you. I appreciate you trying to protect me. Is there something I can do for you?

It may say nothing, or it may give you some very specific instructions. Follow the guidance and soothe this part of yourself.

Step 3: Point to the Evidence

It also helps me to remember that I've lived through this difficult cycle, or at least a similar one, before. And guess what? I'm still here. You've lived through many, many cycles and thousands of transits, and since you're reading this, you're still here too. You are resilient.

Step 4: Flip the Script

Even as a professional astrologer, the cycles that I think are going to be the "worst ever" can manifest in a way I didn't expect. And yes, sometimes in a completely bland, unnoticeable way. Instead of assuming something in astrology is "bad," I prefer to keep my options open and assume it's going to enhance my life. Brainstorm and think about what gifts you could squeeze out of this cycle. Where's the positive here, or at least the neutral?

Step 5: Make a Plan

Instead of the passive approach of waiting on astrology to "do something to you," you can do something to it. Give the astrology a direct channel or pathway to act through. Make a plan, and yes, actually write it out.

Let's pretend Mercury is about to go retrograde. This happens all the time, and it's a great opportunity to practice calming astrology fear. A Mercury retrograde plan might look a little something like this:

Pause and take a breath before saying yes to a new commitment.

Schedule in buffer time before and after appointments so you don't feel rushed.

Review your quarterly goals and make sure they still feel supportive and realistic.

The rest of this book, especially the planet sections, will give you practical plan ideas.

Step 6: Prevention

Do what you can to prevent astrology fear from striking again. Limit how much astrology content you consume, and be really intentional about where it comes from. If it leaves you feeling scared and yucky, it's probably not the source for you.

If astrology fear is your constant companion, I suggest taking a break from tracking the astrology weather for a while and focusing on planet channeling instead (we'll talk about this at length soon). Planet channeling is a journaling process that allows you to receive guidance from the planets without having to know all the details of what's happening up there. This practice can satiate your astrology appetite while also protecting you from potentially activating information.

And finally, something that helps me when astrology fear pops up is to write down or repeat reminders like these:

> This is temporary.
>
> I've already lived through this.
>
> I am capable.
>
> I'm more informed this time around.
>
> I'll keep my options open. I'm open to this unfolding differently than I expect, beyond what my mind can comprehend.
>
> There might be something about this cycle I don't fully grasp or understand.
>
> There are always other cycles happening simultaneously, offering silver linings in the form of mindset shifts, helpful people, and unexpected turns for the better.

Now that you're committed to presence before prediction, let's dive into the fun part and identify your co-creator planet.

two

Your Cosmic Clock

Annual Profections

Your birth chart is like a clock. Until its hour strikes, each planet lies "dormant" or works subtly in the background. It's as if a planet is asleep until the cosmos gives its shoulders a gentle shake. As time moves forward, each planet gets a turn to wake up and do its thing. One way to figure out which planet is taking its turn is an ancient technique called annual profections. This technique dates back thousands of years and was used by Hellenistic, Arabic, and medieval astrologers. One of the main sources for annual profections is a second-century astrologer named Vettius Valens. In book 4 of his *Anthology*, Valens urges all astrologers to give him credit when sharing this technique, lest they be cursed. So, thank you, Valens. And thank you to the teachers who passed it along to me, including Demetra George, Kelly Surtees, and Chris Brennan.

Annual profections was lost for a time and, thanks to a translation project called Project Hindsight, was rediscovered in the 1990s and has been revived and further developed since that time. I'm so grateful that I was introduced to annual profections in my very first year of astrology school. I've used this technique in every consultation since. Profections help me make sense of life.

The word *profection* comes from the Latin *proficiscor*, which means "to depart," "to set out," or "to proceed"; and that's exactly what you're doing here. You have a starting point, and you set out around the astrology chart from there, "turning on" different parts of the chart as you go. In annual profections' simplest form, you profect, or set out from the ascendant (located in the first house of your chart), and move forward one sign/house per year of life. When you have a birthday, you "jump" to the next sign/house. In this way, you move through your chart year by year, house by house, sign by sign, "waking up" different pieces of it and therefore different themes in your life. Pro tip: This technique is best used with whole-sign houses, where one house corresponds with one entire zodiac sign.

Annual profections give you the big brushstrokes for the year ahead by pinpointing your house, sign, and planet of the year (which I call your co-creator in this book). When you know these pieces, you can identify the themes and potentials of your life right now. You'll know what's ripe and ready to flourish and what's taking a back seat.

Although we won't be covering it in this book, I want to note that there's a much more advanced version of annual profections in which you profect from many other points in the chart simultaneously. (Yes, you can profect from almost anything—the Sun, the Moon, the Lot of Fortune, the tenth house, whatever!) It can become quite mind-boggling and complex. What I present in this book is what I find to be the most accurate and helpful in consultation.

• • • • • • •

Step 1: Find Your House of the Year

The basic idea of profections is pretty simple. Each year of your life is linked to a specific house in your birth chart. That house is "activated" or "turned on" for the entire year. It's like walking into a room that's been closed off for a while and flipping on the light switch. That house (or room, in this example) and everything in it is illuminated. That part of your birth chart is now fully awake.

Houses represent different life areas. When a house is activated or awakened, the life areas associated with that house are activated too. They become the focal point for your year and may describe how you spend your time and the major events that may unfold. For example, when you're in a seventh-house year, relationships may be the major focus. When you're in a tenth-house year, career may take most of your attention. When you're in a twelfth-house year, you may feel like taking a step back and reassessing things.

At birth, you begin in a first-house year. When you turn one, you jump to the second house. When you turn two, the cosmic clock comes to the third house. When you turn three, the hour strikes the fourth house, and the pattern repeats around the wheel for your entire life. Simple, right? But it works. Of course, there's way more astrology where this came from, and we'll dive into that soon, but now you have the basic idea.

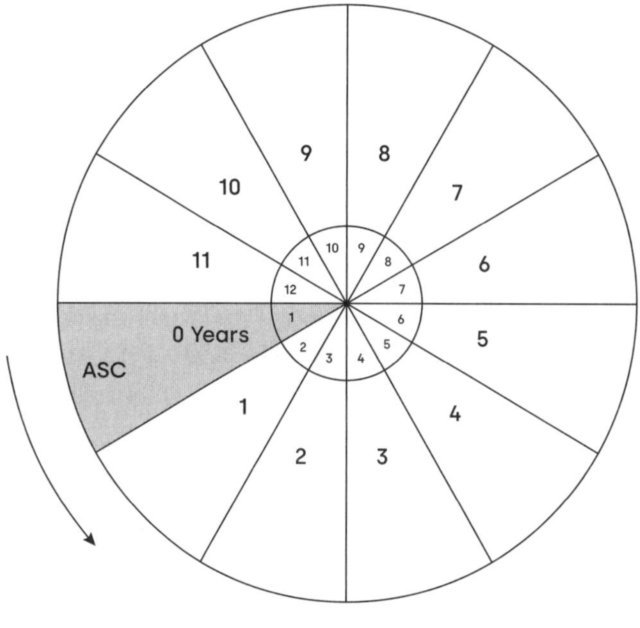

Count profection years beginning at the first house or ascendant (marked as ASC) with birth or year zero and move counterclockwise.

All you need to know to get started with profections is how old you are. (I bet you know that.) Let's pretend you're forty. Starting in the first house with zero, count around the wheel of your chart until you come to your current age. Whatever house you land in is your profected house—let's just call it your house of the year from now on. Or, you can use the following table for quick reference.

House	1st	2nd	3rd	4th	5th	6th	7th	8th	9th	10th	11th	12th
Age	0	1	2	3	4	5	6	7	8	9	10	11
	12	13	14	15	16	17	18	19	20	21	22	23
	24	25	26	27	28	29	30	31	32	33	34	35
	36	37	38	39	40	41	42	43	44	45	46	47
	48	49	50	51	52	53	54	55	56	57	58	59
	60	61	62	63	64	65	66	67	68	69	70	71
	72	73	74	75	76	77	78	79	80	81	82	83
	84	85	86	87	88	89	90	91	92	93	94	95
	96	97	98	99	100	101	102	103	104	105	106	107

Now that you know your house of the year, you know what life themes are likely to be at the top of your mind and perhaps the top of your to-do list this year. Here's a rundown of the houses and the life areas they represent to get you started. We'll dive deeper into them later.

House	Life Area(s) Represented
1st	Life, wellness
2nd	Money
3rd	Siblings, learning, communication
4th	Home, family
5th	Children, creativity
6th	Illness, work
7th	Relationships

8th	Death, shared money (Don't freak out! There's a lot of nuance to this one.)
9th	Spirituality, travel, learning
10th	Career and status
11th	Hopes and dreams, friendships
12th	Suffering (There's lots of nuance to this one too!)

There are a couple of patterns that I want to point out about annual profections before we move on. First, they are twelve-year cycles, each with a beginning and an end. You start a fresh cycle when you come to a first-house year, and you bring that cycle to completion when you come to a twelfth-house year. The transition from a twelfth-house year to a first-house year is really pivotal and tends to coincide with major life transitions too.

Second, there are certain ages of life when similar themes will circle back around. For example, the ages of twenty-five, thirty-seven, forty-nine, sixty-one, seventy-three, and eighty-five are all second-house years. You might notice during these times that you're switching jobs, saving up for a big purchase, exploring retirement, or dealing with your money in another type of way. I like to think of profections as spiraling upward. You may revisit the same part of your chart over and over again, but it's with fresh eyes, more wisdom, and new tools to navigate that part of your life with. There are also other factors, like solar return charts and transits—which we'll get to later—that make one second-house profection year different from another. These extra astrological factors also explain, in part, why everybody's second-house year isn't the same or why everybody turning forty-nine doesn't have an identical money experience.

So, that's the first step. Count around the chart until you land in your house of the year, which corresponds with your age. Ready for more?

Step 2: Identify Your Sign of the Year

It's not just the house of the year that's activated but everything inside the house too. First, there's a zodiac sign occupying that house. Let's pretend that sign is Sagittarius. That makes Sagittarius your sign of the year. This can give you a few clues about how the year may flow and feel. Get to know this sign and its personality. You'll also want to watch planets in the real-time sky as they travel through your sign of the year. These transits (a.k.a. planetary movements) may correlate with some changes or turning points for you. We'll talk more about this later.

Step 3: Find Your Planet of the Year (Your Co-Creator)

So, now you know your house of the year and your sign of the year, but what about your planet of the year? Traditionally, this planet is called your time lord, but remember, I like to think of it as your co-creator. Your co-creator planet informs the tone and quality of time—how it passes, how it feels, and what it brings. It's as if this planet is unlocked, as if it were sleeping and suddenly you get to wake it up and say, "Hey, what do you have in store for me?" This planet is so important that I've devoted most of this book to exploring it. I want you to think of it as your partner or your greatest ally for the year ahead. Just like your highlighted house, your co-creator changes to a new planet on your birthday.

Your co-creator is the planet that's the most activated. Whatever it's in charge of and whatever it represents will be what you're sorting through and working with this year. Every planet in your chart has a job. It manages a handful of life topics and represents certain life events. When that planet is your co-creator, those topics and events come to pass. It's as though planets make promises, and when they get turned on, they make good on their promises. We'll talk about how to determine your co-creator's job in a later chapter.

How do you identify your co-creator? Well, this is where the technique begins to branch off and where different astrologers have different opinions. I'm going to offer you the easiest method first and then an alternative. You get to play with both and determine which resonates with you.

Option 1

To determine your co-creator, you just need to know which planet "rules" your highlighted house and sign of the year. Planets "rule" zodiac signs. Signs are like properties and planets are like landlords. There's one planet that "owns" your sign of the year and highlighted house. It may not be living in the house, but it does have the final say in how things go. It sets the rent, it says who can stay there, and it maintains the property. For example, if Virgo is your sign of the year, Mercury is your co-creator. Or, if Libra is your sign of the year, Venus is your co-creator. Take a moment to find your co-creator in the table below. Also note that the outer planets Uranus, Neptune, and Pluto cannot be co-creators. These planets were discovered many years after annual profections came to be, and in traditional astrology, the outer planets do not rule zodiac signs.

Sign of the Year	Co-Creator (Planet of the Year)
Aries	Mars
Taurus	Venus
Gemini	Mercury
Cancer	Moon
Leo	Sun
Virgo	Mercury
Libra	Venus
Scorpio	Mars
Sagittarius	Jupiter
Capricorn	Saturn
Aquarius	Saturn
Pisces	Jupiter

Option 2

Now for the trickier option. This option comes from our friend Valens. If your house and sign of the year contain a planet, that planet is an alternative co-creator. Let's pretend your house and sign of the year contain Mercury. Well, guess what? Mercury and whatever it represents in your life are turned "on." Any aspects Mercury makes to other planets become primary storylines in your life too.

But what if your house and sign of the year contain multiple planets? Well, those planets all take turns governing the times (remember, we're excluding the outer planets Uranus, Neptune, and Pluto here). It's unclear how much time each planet gets, so you get to play with this. I like to divide the time equally. The planet that's first in zodiacal order goes first, and the planet next in zodiacal order goes second. For example, let's pretend you have Mercury at 17 degrees of Leo and the Sun at 23 degrees of Leo. Mercury comes first (17 is less than 23), so it would govern the times first, and the Sun would be up second.

So which option should you choose? Honestly, I pay attention to both, and if you can hold that much star math in your brain, I suggest you pay attention to both too. The truth is that both co-creators (the one ruling the sign and the one located in the sign) will be activated and important this year.

Step 4 (Optional): Find Your Second (and Maybe Third!) House of the Year

Take a minute to locate your co-creator in your natal chart. If it's not in your house of the year, what other house is it located in? This is your secondary house of the year. However, in my research, I've noticed that this secondary house isn't secondary at all, but equally or even more important than the primary house of the year.

And although not as bright, the lights get turned on in one final place, depending on who your co-creator is. (Pro tip: If your co-creator is the Sun or Moon, this doesn't apply to you. You'll only have one or two houses of the year.) You may have noticed that, other than the Sun and Moon, each planet rules two zodiac signs. You've already identified one of these as your sign of the year, but there's one other sign–house combination that gets lit up as well. These offer additional themes that may arise throughout the year. They usually aren't as obvious, but they can add layers or nuance to your story.

For example, let's pretend that your house of the year is the ninth house, and you have Scorpio in the ninth house and no planets within it.

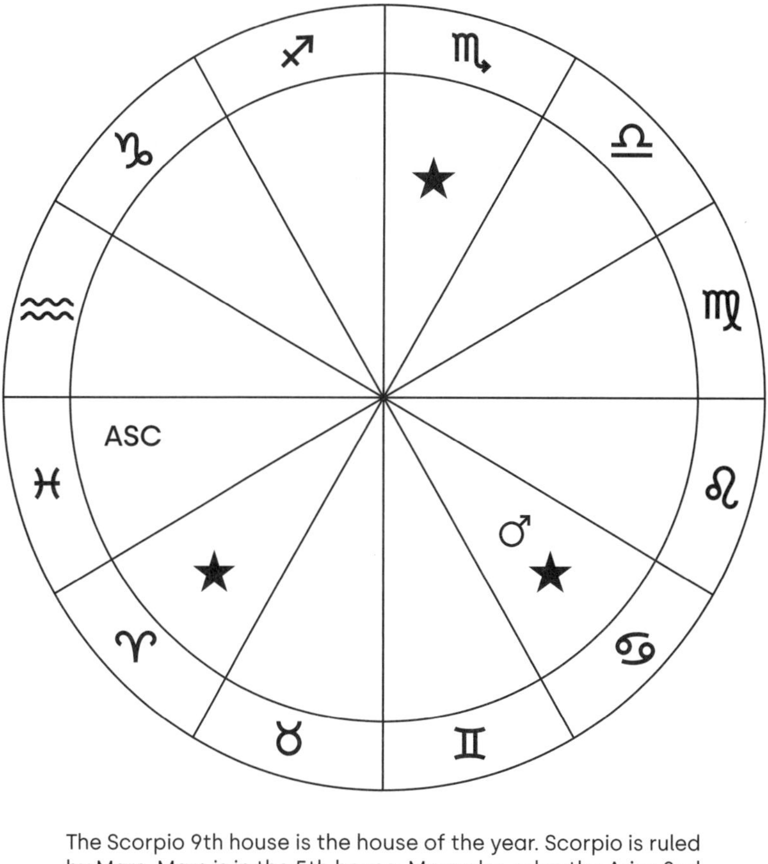

The Scorpio 9th house is the house of the year. Scorpio is ruled by Mars. Mars is in the 5th house. Mars also rules the Aries 2nd house. The houses of the year are the 9th, 5th, and 2nd.

That makes Scorpio your sign of the year. Mars rules Scorpio, which means that Mars is your planet of the year. Let's pretend that your natal Mars is in the fifth house. That means the fifth house is the secondary house of the year. But there's one more step. Scorpio isn't the only sign that Mars rules. It also rules Aries. This means that whatever house Aries occupies (in this example, it would be the second house) is the third house of the year. So, as a recap, the planet of the year is Mars, and the houses of the year are the ninth, fifth, and second.

Your Turn! Figuring Out Your Profection Data

1. How old are you?
2. What house is this age correlated with? That's your house of the year. (Remember to use whole-sign houses for best results.)
3. What zodiac sign occupies this house in your birth chart? That's your sign of the year.
4. What planet rules this zodiac sign? That's your co-creator of the year.
5. Are there any other planets in this sign? That planet(s) is also activated and may act as an alternative co-creator of the year.
6. What house is your co-creator located in? That's your second house of the year.
7. What other zodiac sign does your co-creator planet rule? (This does not apply if your co-creator is the Sun or Moon.)
8. What house does this zodiac sign occupy in your chart? That's your third house of the year.

• • • • • • •

Why Profections Are Important

Other than being ridiculously cool, profections are important for more than a few reasons. Beyond telling you the themes of the year, which planet is your co-creator, and which parts of your chart are turned on, profections tell you what to pay attention to in the sky right now and what to ignore. Have you ever noticed that some Mercury retrogrades are particularly tricky, while others are nothing special? Or that some eclipses bring major shifts, and others just beget a night of tossing and turning? This has to do with profections. Let me explain.

If your co-creator is Mercury, for instance, you better believe Mercury retrograde will be more important for you. If your co-creator is the Sun or Moon, eclipses, New and Full Moons in general, and the Sun's seasonal shifts will be your timekeepers. If Saturn is your co-creator, any big news it's a part of will probably mean big news for you too. Profections act as celestial filtering tools. Just like not everything in your chart is active all the time, not everything happening in the sky will matter to you. No need to think or worry about it. We'll talk more about this when we get to transits.

DIY Profection Project

The best way to learn about profections is to do a personal research project. For this you're going to need either a super-good memory or access to old journals, planners, emails, photos—anything that'll remind you of the major events that occurred during each year of your life. I went through over seventy journals for my DIY Profection Project and in preparation for writing this book. It was a journey. I suggest you start with something more manageable. I recommend starting with your current twelve-year profection cycle because your memories of it will probably be the freshest. This cycle started during your most recent first-house year. That means starting at age twelve, twenty-four, thirty-six, forty-eight, sixty, seventy-two, or eighty-four.

You can print out a blank astrology wheel if you're more visual, create a document if you're more linear, or do both like I do. Head to www.astrologywithclaire.com/cosmicyear to download some DIY Profection Project templates.

If you're using a wheel, begin by writing the ages on the outside of each corresponding house, along with the dates of each of the twelve profection years. For example, let's pretend your birthday is October 7, 1980. That means your first profection year lasted from October 7, 1980, to October 6, 1981. Continue this around the rest of the wheel counterclockwise. If you're doing this in a document, simply create a new bulleted list for each profection year, labeling the top of each list with the corresponding age, house, and dates.

Now, just fill in the details. If you're using a blank astrology wheel, fill in each "pie piece" with the year's main events. What happened each year? Think big picture, milestone events. For example: I got married. I graduated from college. My sister was born. I got fired. I had a child. I was in an accident. I met my best friend. I went through the worst breakup of my life. I got a promotion. I found astrology. I had a spiritual awakening. Be honest, but don't forget to record the good stuff along with the "bad." It's easy to have a negativity bias in astrology, and it's easy to remember the most painful parts of our lives with more clarity—this is human. But even if it takes a little more digging, record the happy stuff too.

Then, get a little more granular. Where were you working? Where were you living and with whom? (I like to put where I was living because I move a lot.) What was taking up most of your time and energy? What were you feeling like physically and emotionally? Maybe you even want to put a picture of yourself next to each profection year so that you can have an even greater connection to that version of you.

Now, take a step back. Do you see any correlations between the house meanings and the main themes of your years? Fascinating, right?! If you don't, that's okay; we have a lot more astrology to go through, and now you have all the data you need in one place. If you're feeling inspired, fill out another wheel or another set of twelve lists so that you can make side-by-side comparisons. For example, put all your seventh-house years in a row and prepare to be amazed.

• • • • • • • •

Okay, great work! That was a lot of high-level astrology. Now that you know who your co-creator is, let's get to know it a little bit better. In the next chapter, I will walk you through a checklist to help you learn how your co-creator operates in your natal chart. Remember how I said each planet has a collection of jobs to do? Well, the next chapter helps you figure out what those jobs are.

three

Astrology in One Chapter

In order for this book to really land and be useful, there are a few things you need to know about astrology first. In order to know what's awake and activated in your birth chart and how to make meaningful statements about it, you have to know what it means in the first place—what it promises, what it signifies, and what its potential is. You have to be able to answer the question *What is this?* to understand how it'll operate when it's "switched on." In this chapter, I offer a method for getting to know any planet in your birth chart on an intimate level. Now that you know who your co-creator planet is, I suggest starting with that.

So, settle in and grab something to write with and something to sip, because we're about to do some major astrology together. I'm going to be very ambitious and do my best to explain traditional astrology (what I practice, with a modern spin) to you in just a few pages. In light of that, this section comes with a few warnings:

- There's always more astrology where this came from. People write tomes on the history and mechanics of astrology and how it works. This is just a crash course. There's a lot missing from this chapter, but I want to give you the most vital bullet points so that you can get started right away.

- I'm not going to sugarcoat anything. I'm very blunt in these pages, which is awkward for me. I'm a sweetheart. But in order for you to learn real astrology quickly, we need to take it down to its simplest form, and that means dropping a lot of nuance—just for now. We'll add the nuance and round edges back in for the rest of the book.

  Traditional astrology is very clear that certain planets are "good" and certain planets are "bad." It doesn't shy away from the fact that suffering exists, and it allows the planets, houses, and other astrological details to describe the full spectrum of the human experience. We've all lived through seasons of joy and seasons of suffering, and in order for astrology to be accurate, it must be allowed to describe all of these things. This can be hard to swallow if you're already struggling with a high level of fear in life, but it can actually be really helpful when you're learning. And in this chapter, we're learning.
- Astrology isn't (just) a personality profile. One of the biggest reframes I want to offer is that astrology isn't a personality quiz. Sure, astrology can tell you about your character, how you communicate, how you give and receive love, and so on. But from an ancient lens, astrology is more a map of your life's potential—a map of its events and how certain areas of your life will feel and unfold. As you go through this chapter, try to lift the personality burden off your chart a little bit and lean into more tangible, practical interpretations.

You're going to need a copy of your birth chart to follow along with this chapter. I'm skipping a lot of explanation here, but I highly suggest getting a birth chart with whole-sign houses. That's the house system that most of these techniques were originally based on, and bonus, it's a lot easier on the eyes. As I mentioned earlier, I include recommendations in the "Resources" section in the back of the book that can provide you with a copy of your chart.

Okay. Ready? Let's start at the beginning.

The Planets

Move over, zodiac signs! The most important place to begin is with the planets. I like to imagine the planets as people with specific roles or jobs in your life. You could also think of them as managers of different life departments. Here's a quick summary of each planet's job:

Sun: To individuate, awaken, enliven, illuminate, and stabilize

Moon: To feel, nourish, take care of, and fluctuate

Mercury: To communicate, think, process, speak, write, and learn

Venus: To love, relate, beautify, enjoy, harmonize, and attract

Mars: To act, motivate, work, compete, energize, defend, and divide

Jupiter: To elevate, enrich, grow, improve, and support

Saturn: To ground, endure, limit, separate, and mature

These are the general jobs that each planet does for everyone. But the planets also have very unique and specific jobs for *you* depending on how your birth chart is set up. For example, Venus may generally represent love and affection, but Mercury might actually be your main relationship planet. These personal jobs are determined by the twelve houses, which, as we saw in chapter 2, represent specific areas of life. We'll go into the houses in depth later in the book, but for now, take a look back at the list on page 16 if you need a refresher.

When using the whole-sign house system, one zodiac sign corresponds to one house. And, long story short, since each planet rules a zodiac sign or two, it also rules or oversees the corresponding house and its life area. For example, let's pretend the sign of Virgo corresponds to your seventh house. That means Mercury, which rules Virgo, is your primary relationship planet.

Take a minute to write out the jobs your co-creator planet does in your life using the following prompt. If you need a reminder of the signs and their traditional ruling planets, you can refer to the table on page 19.

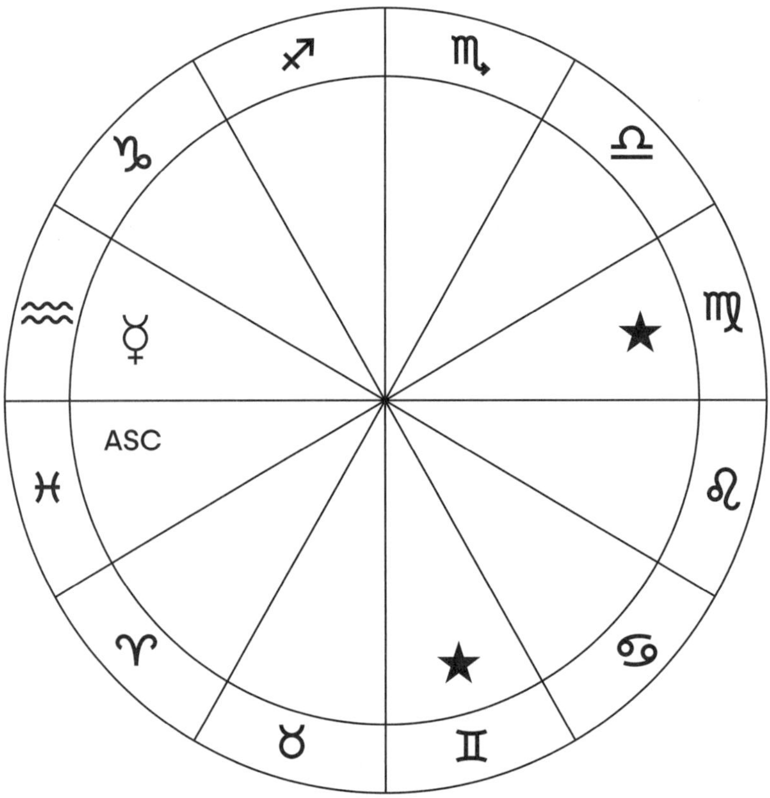

Mercury rules Gemini and Virgo. In this chart, that means Mercury manages the 7th house of relationships as well as the 4th house of home and family.

[Planet]'s innate jobs are to [jobs]. In my life, [planet] also manages [house topics based on sign rulership].

Example: Mercury's innate jobs are to communicate, think, process, speak, write, and learn. In my life, Mercury also manages relationships, home, and family.

The CLEAR Method for Assessing Your Co-Creator

Now that you know your co-creator's jobs, it's time to get real about its performance. How well does it do its job? This is important because it will also help you figure out how your current year may feel. If a planet with poor job performance gets activated, the year tends to bring a few bumps. If a planet with excellent job performance gets activated, the year tends to bring blessings and upgrades. When you can assess a planet objectively, you can view your life honestly and make a plan to be present for both the joys and the challenges.

To help you assess your planet's job performance, I've created a mnemonic: CLEAR. CLEAR stands for club, location, energy, appearance, and relationships. This is a simplification of something called planetary condition, a collection of ancient techniques used to assess the "happiness" and therefore effectiveness of a planet. It's basically a checklist where you determine if a planet can express itself fully and easily. Planets that express themselves easily do what they say they're going to do.

The CLEAR method can be used to evaluate your co-creator in both your natal chart and your solar return chart, which is the chart for your most recent birthday. Your natal co-creator will tell you the baseline of what to expect this year, and your solar return co-creator will tell you whether or not to expect better or worse than baseline. We'll address solar return charts at the end of the book.

C: Club

The first thing you want to know is what club your co-creator is a part of—the day club or the night club. In traditional astrology this is called its sect, but thinking of it as a club is more fun. A sect, or club, refers to a group of planets with shared interests and priorities. The day club is led by the Sun, and its members are Jupiter and Saturn. The night club is led by the Moon, and its members are Venus and Mars. Mercury can be part of either club (more on this later). When your co-creator is part of the right club, it's with its friends, and it has support—in other words, it's a check in the I-can-do-good-work-for-you column.

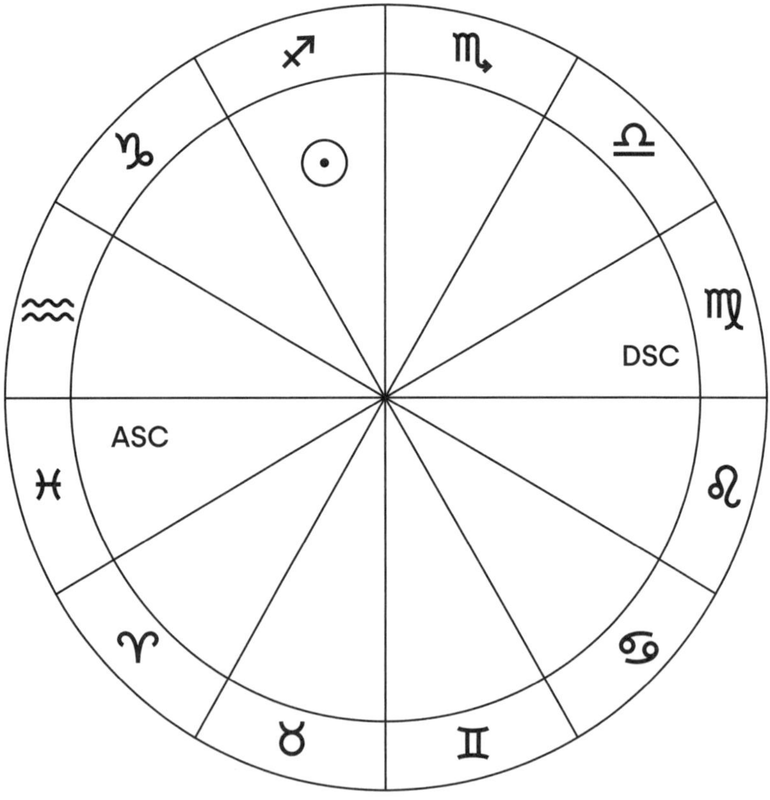

The Sun is above the horizon, making this a day chart.

Which club is the "right" club? That depends on when you were born. If you were born during the day, you're part of the day club. If you were born at night, you're part of the night club. To be precise, draw a line from your ascendant degree to your descendant degree. That's the horizon. If your Sun is above the horizon line, you have a day chart and are part of the day club. If your Sun is below the horizon line, you have a night chart and are part of the night club. In an ideal scenario, your co-creator will be a part of the same club as you.

When your co-creator is part of the same club as you, it has a base level of comfort. You two are already familiar with each other.

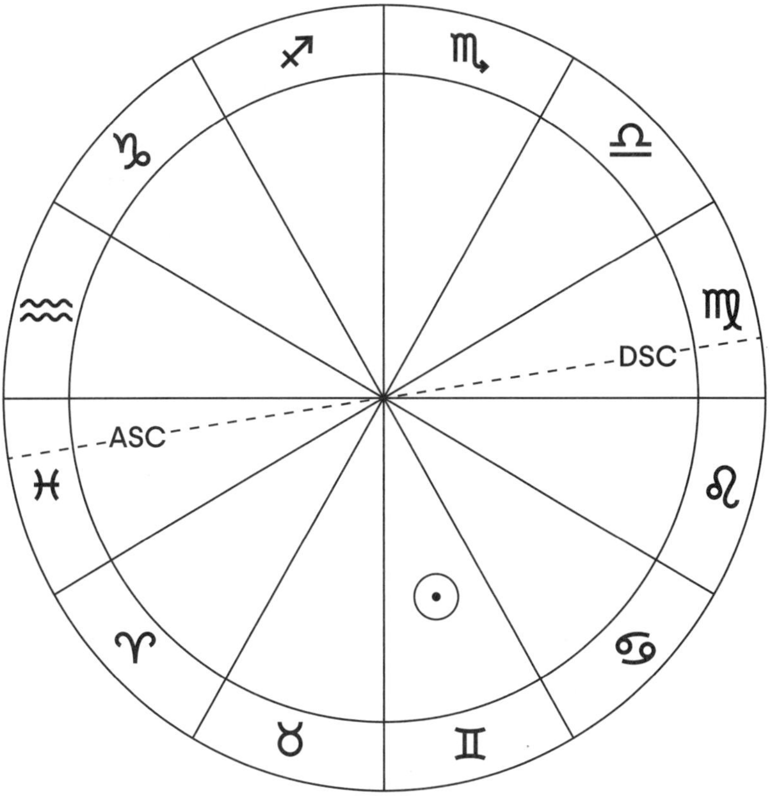

The Sun is below the horizon, making this a night chart.

If your co-creator is from the opposite club, things may feel a little awkward, and you may be asked to work with concepts and themes that are outside your comfort zone. It's like your co-creator planet has a guest pass, but it doesn't have access to all the bells and whistles that a full-blown member has. It can still operate and do its work, but it's going to have to adjust its normal *modus operandi* for something a little less natural. But it can get used to it, and so can you.

Let's flesh this out with an example. Let's pretend you have a night chart and your co-creator for the year is the Moon. Nice. You're already led by the Moon in your daily life since it's the club leader of your chart naturally. You're already led by feeling, sensation, and instinct. You already prioritize fluctuation and use your intuitive sense to make decisions. So, having the Moon as your co-creator is a check in the I-know-this column. But what if the Sun is your co-creator? This isn't bad; it's just different. Being led by the Sun may be quite foreign for a night-chart person. The Sun is about climbing to the highest place, being led by the mind or the intellect and by what it can see instead of what it can feel. The Sun wants to achieve. Can you work with a co-creator like this as a night-chart person? Of course! But there will be a learning curve. So, this is a check in the this-is-new column. New is not negative. It just requires some creativity and adaptability.

Extra Step If Your Co-Creator Is Mercury

Leave it to Mercury to be extra tricky. If your planet of the year is Mercury, you have one extra step to determine what club it's a part of.

Find the Sun in your chart. Draw a line through the chart from the Sun to the other side. Turn your chart so that it appears as if your Sun is on the ascendant, rising up over the horizon (moving clockwise). Now find Mercury. Is Mercury above the line or below the line? In other words, is Mercury ahead of the Sun or behind the Sun? If Mercury is above the line, or rising before the Sun, it's part of the day club. If Mercury is below the line, or rising after the Sun, it's part of the night club.

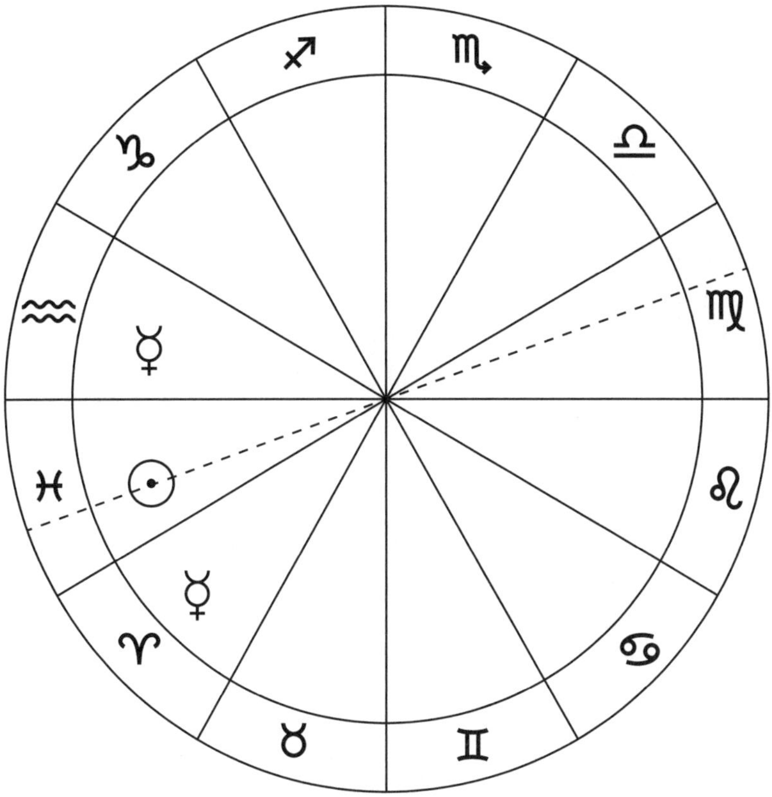

The "day club" Mercury is above the line.
The "night club" Mercury is below the line.

Take a minute to determine the club of your chart and your co-creator using the prompt below.

I have a [day/night] chart. My co-creator [planet] is in the [day/night] club. This is a [match/mismatch].

Example: I have a day chart. My co-creator Mars is in the night club. This is a mismatch.

Benefic or Malefic?

There are two other clubs that planets can belong to, and these are the benefic or the malefic clubs. Breathe. These words may sound scary, but it's really important that we keep them around. Again, in order for astrology to be both helpful and accurate, it needs to be able to describe the full breadth of human experience, and that includes both joy and suffering. By classifying the planets into their basic natures of acting in a beneficial or challenging way, we can make sense of what we've lived through in the past and look at our present with more context. We all have parts of life that are a little crunchy and that cause us some pain.

Benefic planets are life-affirming. Their actions are to grow, expand, reward, connect, honor, and begin. If your co-creator is a benefic planet, you're starting from a pretty good place. The benefic planets are Jupiter and Venus.

Malefic planets are life-stifling. Their actions are to block, thwart, challenge, isolate, inflame, and end. If your co-creator is a malefic planet, you may have some obstacles to overcome. The malefic planets are Saturn and Mars.

Mercury is said to be "common," meaning it can be malefic or benefic depending on the greater context. If it's close to a benefic planet, Venus or Jupiter, it tends to act like a benefic. If it's close to a malefic planet, Mars or Saturn, it tends to act like a malefic.

The Sun and Moon are called luminaries, and they aren't traditionally given malefic or benefic labels, but in my experience, they tend to act like functional benefics.

Depending on when you were born, one benefic planet is more powerful for you, and one malefic planet is more challenging for you. Here's the cheat sheet: If you were born during the day, your most helpful planet is Jupiter, and your most challenging planet is Mars. If you were born at night, your most helpful planet is Venus, and your most challenging planet is Saturn.

Extremely Blunt, Unsugarcoated Summary

Day Chart	Night Chart
Jupiter: The great	Venus: The great
Venus: The good	Jupiter: The good
Saturn: The bad	Mars: The bad
Mars: The ugly	Saturn: The ugly

Now we can make a sweeping generalization about an entire year based on whether its ruling planet is benefic or malefic. If you're in a year directed by your most powerful benefic, it's more likely that the better things in life will manifest. Of course there are exceptions, but for the most part, we can say that the current time is generally life-affirming, filled with opportunity and things that spur you on.

On the other hand, if your current year is governed by a malefic planet—especially your most challenging malefic—you have a clue that things may be a bit more of a battle. And here comes a little sugarcoating, despite what the heading says above, because I can't help it. Are malefics always and only bad? No. They operate on a wide spectrum. A malefic planet in a good position can actually do good in your life. Plus, without resistance or challenge in life, we would never have the experience of victory or overcoming. We would never push or stretch ourselves. In their own way, malefics encourage us to reach for something better and to heal.

Continue applying the CLEAR method to your co-creator with the simple prompt below.

My co-creator [planet] is [a benefic/a malefic/common/a luminary]. It's naturally [life-affirming/life-stifling], but there's always nuance to this.

Example: My co-creator Jupiter is a benefic. It's naturally life-affirming, but there's always nuance to this.

L: Location

Your co-creator is placed in a very specific part of your natal chart and your solar return chart. It has a unique "address," a.k.a. a zodiac sign and house. Just like you have favorite places to hang out or visit, planets also have their preferred locales. And just like your job performance might be affected by your environment, a planet's ability to do good work for you hinges on its sign and house placement.

The Zodiac Signs

A planet's zodiac sign affects how it expresses. I like to think of a zodiac sign as a photo filter, which may change how you look or add something funny to your face in the photo, but it's still a picture of you. It's the same thing with the planets. A planet is always itself, but it takes on a certain tone based on the sign it's being filtered through. For example, Mars will always be Mars, but it might use a Gemini filter. It's still going to do Mars things but in a Gemini way.

Remember, we're lifting the personality burden off of the chart, and we're expanding it to be a map of your life's potential. So try not to get stuck asking, *What does X planet in X sign say about my personality?* and think more about, *What does X planet in X sign say about its job performance?*

Zodiac signs are classified in numerous ways, but here we're just going to focus on two: gender (also called polarity) and mode.

Gender

The gender, or polarity (i.e., masculine or feminine), of a zodiac sign describes its pace as well as its orientation. Is it more outward-facing or inward-facing? The mode of a zodiac sign (cardinal, fixed, or mutable) gives us a better idea of how a sign moves and behaves.

Masculine, outward (a.k.a. yang) signs are either Fire signs (Aries, Leo, and Sagittarius) or Air signs (Gemini, Libra, and Aquarius).

When a planet is in a masculine sign, it's more external, extroverted, active, and quick.

Feminine, inward (a.k.a. yin) signs are Earth signs (Taurus, Virgo, and Capricorn) or Water signs (Cancer, Scorpio, and Pisces). When a planet is in a feminine sign, it's more internal, introverted, passive, and slow.

Let's take an example. Mars's job is always to act, but the way it's going to do that depends on where it is in the zodiac. If Mars is in a masculine sign like Aries, it's going to do its acting in a bold way. It may take action without really thinking or processing beforehand. Is Mars in a feminine sign just going to sit on its hands? Of course not! Acting is what Mars does, but it's going to potentially take more time to form an action plan. It's probably going to check in with itself before it does anything, and it might be a bit more hesitant to step out.

Take a minute to add to your co-creator narrative by filling out the prompt below.

My co-creator is in the sign of [zodiac sign here]. This is a [masculine/feminine] sign, which means my co-creator is more likely to be [extroverted/introverted, active/passive] and [fast/slow].

Example: My co-creator is in the sign of Aries. This is a masculine sign, which means my co-creator is more likely to be extroverted, active, and fast.

Mode

Another thing that informs how a planet will do its job is the modality, or mode, of the zodiac sign it's placed in. I like to think of mode as a mode of operation. It describes *how* a planet does its job along with any strengths or challenges. The three modes are cardinal, fixed, and mutable, and they're based on the seasonal wheel.

Cardinal signs correlate with the months that start a new season. They overlap with the solstices and equinoxes. The cardinal signs are Aries, Cancer, Libra, and Capricorn. Planets in these signs excel at starting things and move in a forceful, initiating way.

Fixed signs correlate with the height of a season, where it's in full swing. The fixed signs are Taurus, Leo, Scorpio, and Aquarius. Planets in fixed signs move in a steady and consistent way. Come hell or high water, they're going to bring something to completion, even if it's not in their best interest.

Mutable signs correlate with the months when the seasons are beginning to shift from one to the next. The mutable signs are Gemini, Virgo, Sagittarius, and Pisces. Planets in mutable signs are excellent at adapting and pivoting and tend to do their thing in a meandering way.

Continue your co-creator narrative with the prompt below.

My co-creator is in a [cardinal/fixed/mutable] sign. This means that it does its job in a [forceful/steady/meandering] way.

Example: My co-creator is in a cardinal sign. This means that it does its job in a forceful way.

Special Conditions

There are zodiac signs that are especially supportive or especially repellent to certain planets. A planet's job performance can be greatly enhanced or inhibited if it finds itself in one of these extreme environments. Keep in mind that this section won't apply to everyone. Use the table below to see if it applies to you. If your co-creator isn't in one of these extreme places, no big deal; that's pretty normal!

At the top of the list of a planet's favorite places is its domicile, the sign that it rules, which is its ideal working environment. It's like the planet is at home there. When you're at home, you're surrounded by your creature comforts and your favorite things. You know how to work the remote and turn on the air conditioning, and you can walk around in your underwear, or less, if you want to. When you're at home, you're in charge. It's the same with a planet in its own sign. If your co-creator is in the sign that it rules, its job performance should be tip-top.

Opposite the sign a planet owns is the sign of its detriment, but you can think of it as being as far away from home as you can imagine. I like to think of a planet in detriment as someone landing in a foreign country, where they don't speak the language, they don't have the right currency, they don't know anybody, and oh yeah, their luggage got lost so they don't even have a toothbrush. That's not the end of the world, but it's a pretty tough spot. Planets in detriment don't have a lot of resources. They're not in charge. They have to be really creative about how they get from A to B. If your co-creator is in detriment, things this year may take more time, may feel unstable, or may need outside help.

Another place a planet loves to be is in the sign of its exaltation. This is like being invited as an honored guest to someone's villa. You may not own the place, but they put you in the best room, cook all your meals, and take you on tours. It's almost better than owning the place because you're not in charge of the upkeep. You just get to enjoy being taken care of. A planet in exaltation is literally high above. It's like being put on a pedestal. It has respect and praise, it's well liked, it's popular, and it's confident. If your co-creator is exalted, it probably has some great stuff in store for you this year, if it can get off the chaise lounge.

Opposite the sign of a planet's exaltation is the sign of its fall. I like to think of this as a planet rushing off to work with its hands full, taking a tumble, and landing in a puddle. Well, that *is* annoying. Now its shirt has a coffee stain on it, and its reports are drenched. It still makes it to the meeting, but it looks a little disheveled, and it's kind of embarrassing that the reports are all wet. A planet in fall has literally fallen from a high place to a low place. It may represent starting from the bottom or being knocked down a peg. When a co-creator is in fall, its job performance can be limited, but you have a unique opportunity to obtain a beginner's mind, to embrace humility, and to help others stand back up too. The table below shows each planet's domicile, detriment, exaltation, and fall signs.

Planet	Domicile/ Rulership	Detriment	Exaltation	Fall
Sun	Leo	Aquarius	Aries	Libra
Moon	Cancer	Capricorn	Taurus	Scorpio
Mercury	Gemini and Virgo	Sagittarius and Pisces	Virgo	Pisces
Venus	Taurus and Libra	Scorpio and Aries	Pisces	Virgo
Mars	Aries and Scorpio	Libra and Taurus	Capricorn	Cancer
Jupiter	Sagittarius and Pisces	Gemini and Virgo	Cancer	Capricorn
Saturn	Capricorn and Aquarius	Cancer and Leo	Libra	Aries

If you have a co-creator in one of these special positions, fill out the prompt below.

My co-creator is in an extreme position. It's in the sign of its [rulership/detriment/exaltation/fall]. This may [enhance/inhibit] its job performance.

Example: My co-creator is in an extreme position. It's in the sign of its exaltation. This may enhance its job performance.

The Houses

Location also refers to a planet's placement in one of the twelve houses. I like to think of the houses as vacation rentals that are fully furnished. There's a planet that owns the rental (the ruler), and there's a planet that lives in the rental (the occupant). When a planet is in a house (occupant), it has to use the furnishings, resources, and supplies in that house to do its work.

Let's pretend Mercury is renting a space. Mercury's job is to communicate. It really needs a desk and high-speed internet. It would also prefer a corner lot or a balcony so it can go out and announce the news to the townspeople. But maybe it's tucked away in the twelfth house. This rental is off the beaten path and isolated—no phones or internet here, folks. Does Mercury still communicate? Yes, but it has to use twelfth-house things to do it, or it might communicate about twelfth-house topics. The house that your co-creator is located in represents the life topics that it must use to express itself.

Angularity

Just like some planets are benefic or malefic, some houses are considered strong or weak, favorable or unfavorable. Let's talk about strength first. Angularity is part of what determines whether a house is strong or weak and therefore if a planet in that house has the power to do its job effectively. Understanding angularity can help you grasp why certain years stand out and why others aren't much to write home about.

A house can be angular, succedent, or cadent. You can think of the houses like a hill. At the top of the hill is the angular house. From way up there you have a great view, and the ground is steady. Going uphill toward the top is the role of the succedent house, and going downhill away from the top is the role of the cadent house.

Angular Houses: 1, 4, 7, 10

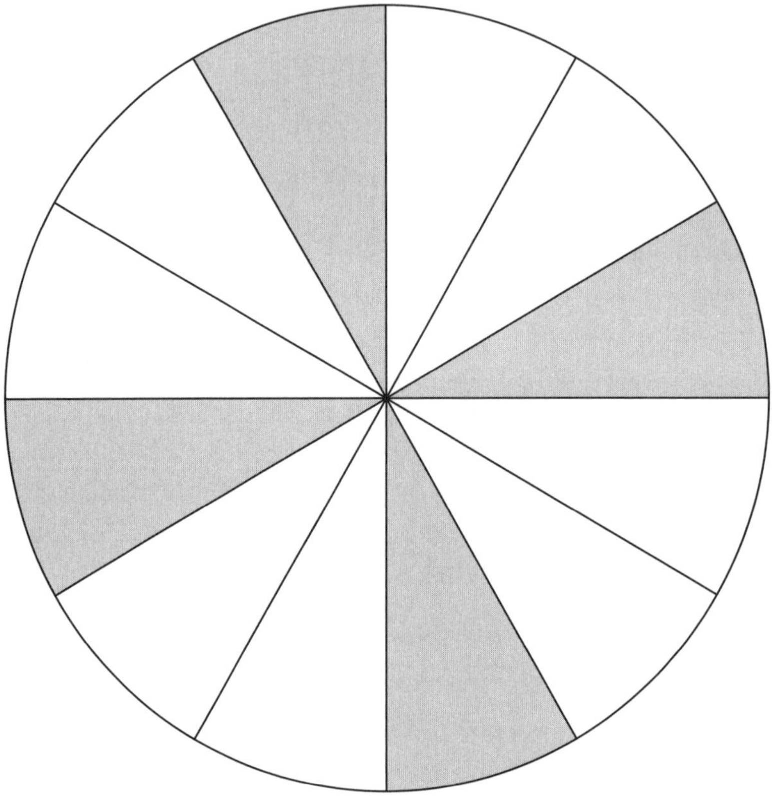

The angular houses are 1, 4, 7, and 10.

Just like the solstices and equinoxes are the four turning points of the year, the angular houses are the four turning points of the day. If you draw a line from the ascendant to the descendant, or the first house to the seventh house, you get the horizon. The Sun's daily journey through the sky is where these houses get their names: Rising, Midheaven, Setting, and Subterranean. The Sun rises, it comes to its highest point, it sets, and it comes to its lowest point beneath the earth. (Side note: A planet's diurnal motion in the chart is clockwise, but its zodiacal motion is counterclockwise.)

The four angular houses of the chart, like the four cardinal directions and the four seasons, are primary. They're page-turners. They make your world go 'round. They have a firm grip on the wheel of your life, meaning they have the most influence and power. A co-creator in an angular house is considered strong, influential, and effective. And although it's not a hard rule, during times when the angular houses are highlighted, larger events or chapters of life tend to unfold. For example, it might be a year when a big milestone happens or when something you've been working on finally sees the light of day.

Succedent Houses: 2, 5, 8, 11

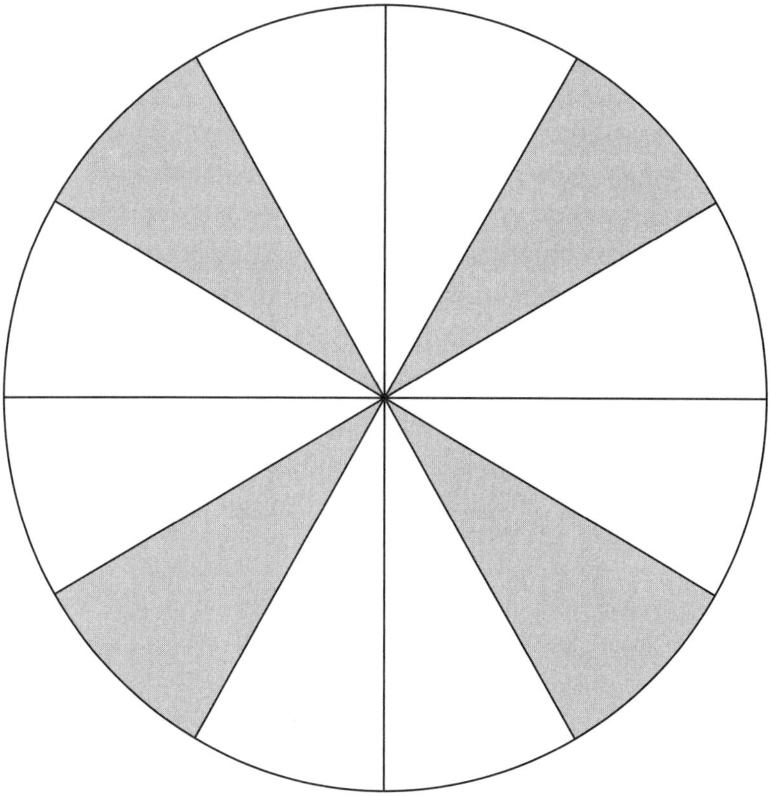

The succedent houses are 2, 5, 8, and 11.

In terms of strength, succedent houses are next in line after the angular houses. They're not as powerful as angular houses, but they're not too shabby. Succedent houses are rising up toward the angular houses. In our hill analogy, they're on the way to the top. A co-creator in a succedent house is considered to be middle of the road in strength. It may not have A+ effort, but it still gets the job done.

Cadent Houses: 3, 6, 9, 12

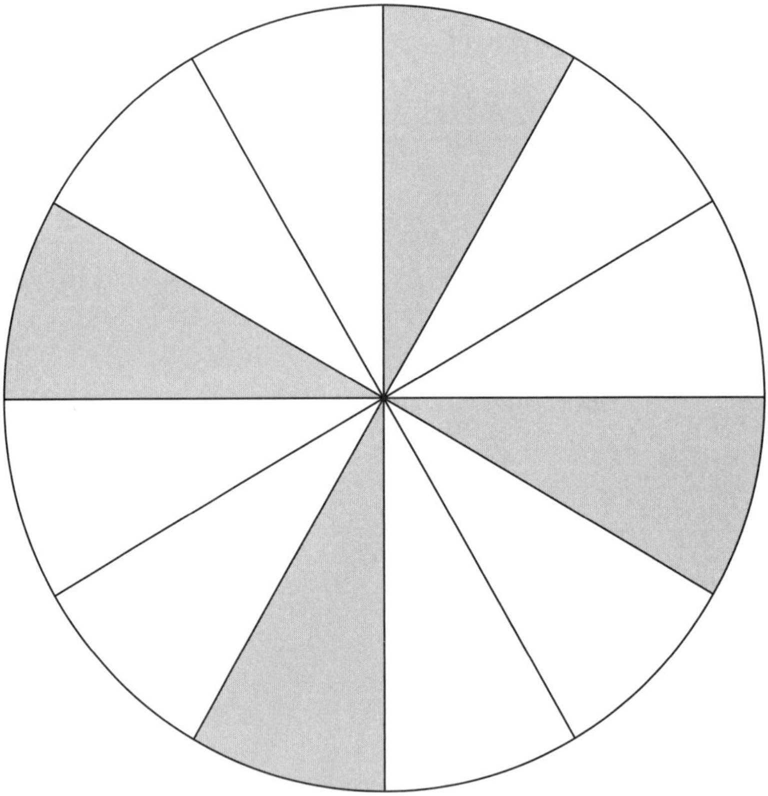

The cadent houses are 3, 6, 9, and 12.

The word *cadent* means "falling," like falling away from something. Cadent houses are unstable and wobbly. In terms of angularity, cadent houses have the least firm grip on the wheel of life and are considered weak. A co-creator in a cadent house doesn't have a lot of *oomph* or power to do its work. It doesn't have stable footing on the steep, downhill slope.

Favorability

Houses can also be considered favorable or unfavorable, but I like to think of them as bright or shady. Does this house get lots of natural light, or is it tucked away in the woods? When a planet is in a bright house, it can see clearly, it is recognized by others, and it is generally more effective at its job. In a bright house, a planet's outcomes or efforts also tend to be more visible or pivotal. The bright houses are first, third, fourth, fifth, seventh, ninth, tenth, and eleventh.

When a planet is in a shady house, it may struggle to do its job efficiently or optimally. It can still do stuff, but it might have different priorities. Instead of driving you to the top of your career or to your person or to your dream home, it might be taking you to places like your mental health or your spiritual health—things that are super important but not super visible. The shady houses are second, sixth, eighth, and twelfth.

Using the information above and the abbreviated house meanings on page 16, complete the prompt below.

My co-creator is located in the [house number] house. [Planet] must use the topic(s) of [house topics] to express itself and do its work. This house is [angular/succedent/cadent] and considered to be a [strong/average/weak] place. This house is [bright/shady] and brings outcomes that are more [visible/invisible] and [worldly/spiritual].

Example: My co-creator is located in the twelfth house. Mercury must use the topic of suffering to express itself and do its work. This house is cadent and considered to be a weak place. This house is shady and brings outcomes that are more invisible and spiritual.

E: Energy

Energy refers to a planet's speed and direction. If a co-creator is traveling quickly, what it wants to do will come about quickly too. The events of the year have fewer obstacles and just happen with more speed. If a co-creator is moving at an average speed, then its natural expression takes over. If a co-creator is moving slower than average, its outcomes and creations will take a more meandering pace. Again, fast isn't "good" and slow isn't "bad." "Bad" things can happen quickly and "good" things can happen slowly and vice versa.

To determine if your co-creator is moving faster or slower than average, you'll need to use software that tells you how fast each planet was moving on the day of your birth. Check the "Resources" section at the back of the book for my recommendation. Then, compare your co-creator's speed in your birth chart to its average speed in the table below. If it moves faster than its average speed, your co-creator is considered fast and energetic. If it's moving slower than its average speed, your co-creator is considered slow and perhaps a little lethargic. Pro tip: If it's retrograde, it's moving slower than average.

Planet	Average Speed
Moon	13° 10.56"
Sun	0° 59.16"
Mercury	0° 59"
Venus	0° 59"
Mars	0° 31.444"
Jupiter	0° 4.987"
Saturn	0° 2.009"

From Demetra George, *Ancient Astrology in Theory and Practice*, vol. I.

If you can determine your co-creator's speed, continue fleshing out your year's story with the prompt below.

My co-creator is moving [fast/slow] and is more likely to do its work [quickly/gradually].

Example: My co-creator is moving slow and is more likely to do its work gradually.

Energy also refers to what direction your co-creator is traveling. If your co-creator is direct, or moving forward, things will probably unfold as planned and as expected. If your co-creator is retrograde, or traveling backward, things may have a few detours, delays, or tangents. These can be happy tangents or things that distract you from your main focus. Just like being in detriment or fall, a retrograde co-creator is an opportunity to be creatively scrappy and take a unique approach to the task at hand. If your co-creator is retrograde, it will typically have a small *r* or *Rx* next to it.

Your co-creator might not be moving at all, which is called being stationary. This is when a planet pauses before changing direction. This happens at the beginning and end of a retrograde cycle. During this time, a planet hangs out at one place in the zodiac like a plane circling the runway waiting for the go-ahead. When your co-creator is stationary, things can feel very sluggish. It might be a time of pausing or waiting and just being with life as it is right now. That can be super uncomfortable in a culture that's so future-oriented, but a stationary co-creator can also be a gift. A stationary planet is able to sink down deep. It gets to know that one part of the zodiac extremely intimately. This can show up as you being consumed by one particular thing in your life—whether welcome or unwelcome. I also like to think of this as an opportunity to master something. When you come to the same topic over and over again like a stationary planet, you have an opportunity to really refine it. Sure, it's repetitive, but it can be a hidden gem. If your co-creator is stationary, it will typically have a small *s* next to it.

Take a moment to check your co-creator's direction and fill out the prompt below.

[Planet] is [direct/retrograde/stationary], which means things this year are likely to proceed [as expected/with delays].

Example: Mercury is stationary, which means things this year are likely to proceed with delays.

A: Appearance

A planet's visibility can also affect its job performance. Planets can be visible or invisible. When a planet is visible, it's in the light. It can see what's coming, and it doesn't have to guess. It has clarity and direct knowledge. Visible planets have a more public expression. They may bring their work out into the light to be seen, celebrated, and observed by other people. A visible co-creator offers you an opportunity to put yourself out there and to take a more public role or to do things that are more outwardly observable.

When a planet is invisible, it's in the dark. It has to rely on intuition, its felt sense, and gut to move forward. It also might do its work in secret or behind the scenes. When a co-creator can't be seen with the naked eye, it might point to a year when you're focusing on things that are more private and not outwardly observable. An invisible co-creator might be perfect for raising an infant or taking a sabbatical, but it might be challenging for running for public office or putting on an event.

Determining if a planet is visible or invisible takes a little astrological elbow grease so be patient with yourself, and when in doubt, consult a professional. Visibility hinges on a planet's relationship with the Sun. There are two different ways a planet can be invisible. First, if a planet is really close to the Sun, the Sun outshines it and the planet "disappears." This occurs when a planet is within 15 degrees of the Sun on either side.

Second, some planets can be invisible if they're directly opposite the Sun within 7.5 degrees on either side. Note that this doesn't apply to all planets, only Mars, Jupiter, and Saturn.

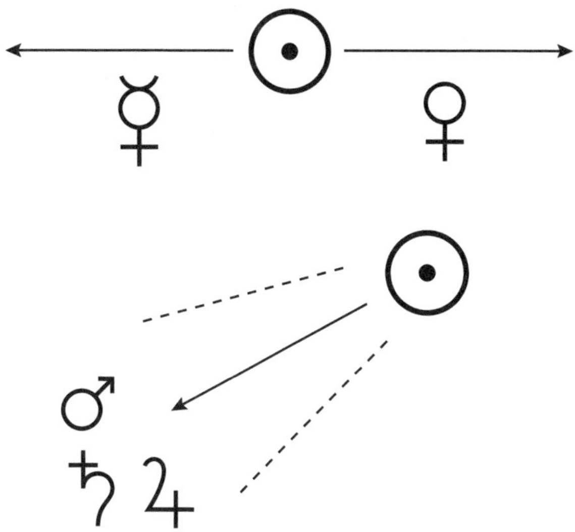

A planet is invisible if it's within 15 degrees of a conjunction with the Sun. Mars, Jupiter, and Saturn are also invisible if they're within 7.5 degrees of an opposition to the Sun.

Continue piecing together your year's narrative with the visibility prompt below.

My co-creator is [visible/invisible] and is likely to do its work in [public/private].

Example: My co-creator is visible and is likely to do its work in public.

R: Relationships

Planets don't act alone; they're part of an intricate network. Just like people, planets have connections with other planets that can be easy and flowing or awkward and strained. Understanding what relationships, called aspects, your co-creator has adds nuance to everything else you've discovered above. It lets you know which other planets you can rely on and whether there's likely to be ease or frustration. Knowing whom your co-creator is talking to can help you gain context and perspective. It can also help you adjust your plans and make them more realistic and compassionate.

To determine what aspects your co-creator makes, you'll need to consult an app or the aspect table on your birth chart. Aspects are a very big topic, so to meet my ambitious goal of explaining astrology in one chapter, I'm going to pare things down a bit. In this book we're using the five traditional aspects: conjunction, opposition, square, trine, and sextile. I also suggest using whole-sign aspects for this activity instead of worrying about orbs and degrees. This will make more sense as we go along.

Conjunctions and Copresence

First, check to see if your co-creator is involved in any conjunctions. A conjunction is when two or more planets cohabitate and share not only the same zodiac sign but the same degree of that zodiac sign. For example, if your natal Mercury is at 13 degrees of Capricorn, and your natal Jupiter is also at 13 degrees of Capricorn, that's a conjunction. But for our purposes with the CLEAR method, I want you to broaden conjunction to the idea of copresence. Copresence is when two planets share the same zodiac sign but aren't necessarily at the same degree. When planets are copresent, they ideally merge their skills and resources together and act as one harmonious entity; but that really depends on whether the two planets get along. Copresence with a

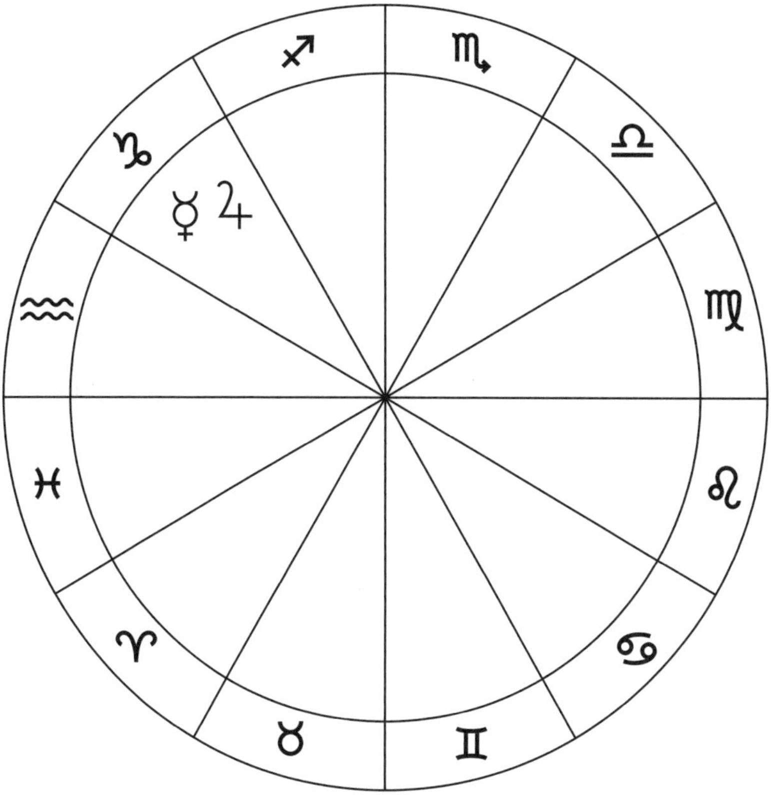

Mercury and Jupiter are conjunct in Capricorn.

benefic planet, Venus or Jupiter, is a real gift, whereas copresence with a malefic planet, Mars or Saturn, can be a bit of a stumbling block.

Oppositions

Next, check to see if your co-creator is involved in any oppositions. Simply look straight across the chart wheel to the opposite sign. If there's a planet there, you have an opposition. For example, if you have Venus in Gemini, the opposite sign is Sagittarius. If Saturn is anywhere in Sagittarius, you have a Venus-Saturn opposition.

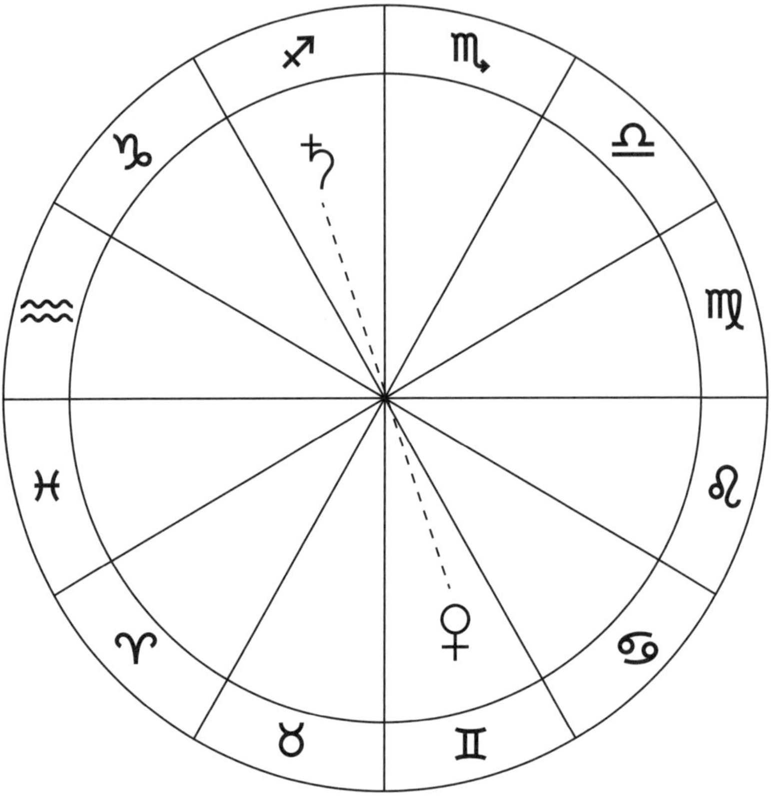

Venus in Gemini opposes Saturn in Sagittarius.

Signs that Oppose

Aries-Libra	Taurus-Scorpio
Gemini-Sagittarius	Cancer-Capricorn
Leo-Aquarius	Virgo-Pisces

An opposition tends to feel like a tug-of-war. Although not always the case, there tends to be two options, two sides, two paths, or some other type of polarity that requires a choice to move forward. Instead of merging together, planets in opposition tend to stand apart and negotiate. They ping emails back and forth trying to nail down the terms of their agreement, or there may be a planetary power struggle. Although it's possible to reach an agreement where both planet parties are happy, it's more realistic that one comes out on top. Just like conjunctions, oppositions from a malefic planet—Mars or Saturn—tend to create difficulty, while oppositions from a benefic planet—Venus or Jupiter—may have a little tension, but I'd take either one any day of the week.

Squares

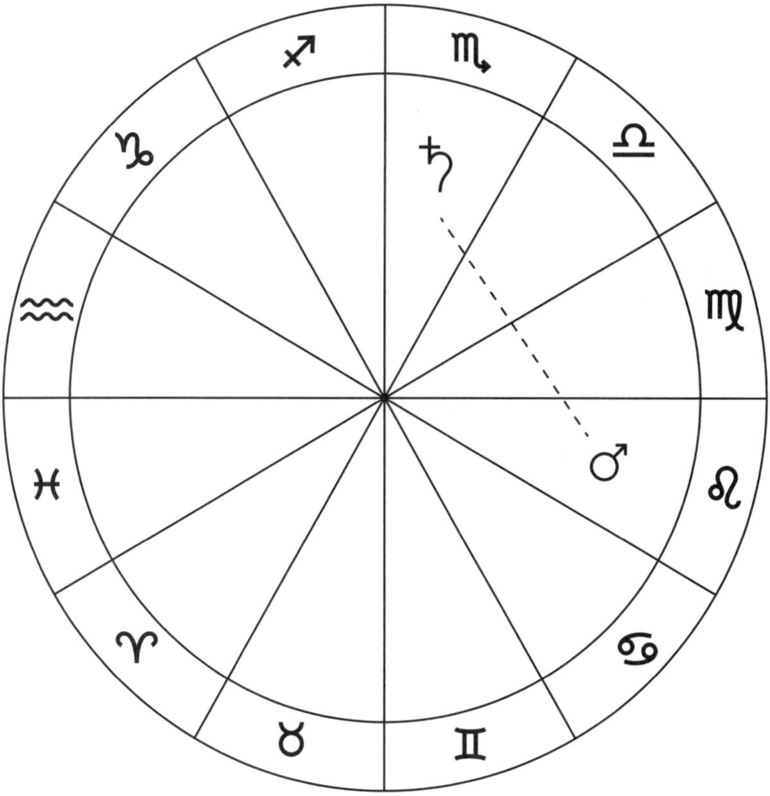

Mars in Leo squares Saturn in Scorpio.

Next, check if your co-creator is involved in any squares. A square occurs when planets make a 90-degree angle. Fun fact: Remember the modes? Signs of the same mode square each other. For example, if your natal Saturn is in Scorpio and your natal Mars is in Leo, they would create a square. Scorpio and Leo are both fixed signs.

Signs that Square

Aries squares Cancer and Capricorn

Taurus squares Leo and Aquarius

Gemini squares Virgo and Pisces

Cancer squares Aries and Libra

Leo squares Taurus and Scorpio

Virgo squares Gemini and Sagittarius

Libra squares Cancer and Capricorn

Scorpio squares Leo and Aquarius

Sagittarius squares Virgo and Pisces

Capricorn squares Aries and Libra

Aquarius squares Scorpio and Taurus

Pisces squares Gemini and Sagittarius

I like to imagine planets in square as two people sitting down for a creative problem-solving session. Instead of sitting across from each other like an opposition, or next to each other like a conjunction, these planets uncomfortably straddle the corner of the table and lean over the same computer trying to figure out how to fix the issue. An opposition can occasionally feel like a stalemate. This is not that. A square is extremely dynamic. It is two planets very engaged in overcoming a conflict or challenge. A square from a malefic planet—Mars or Saturn—can create some issues for your co-creator. But a square from a benefic planet—Venus or Jupiter—is rarely, if ever, experienced as difficult.

Trines

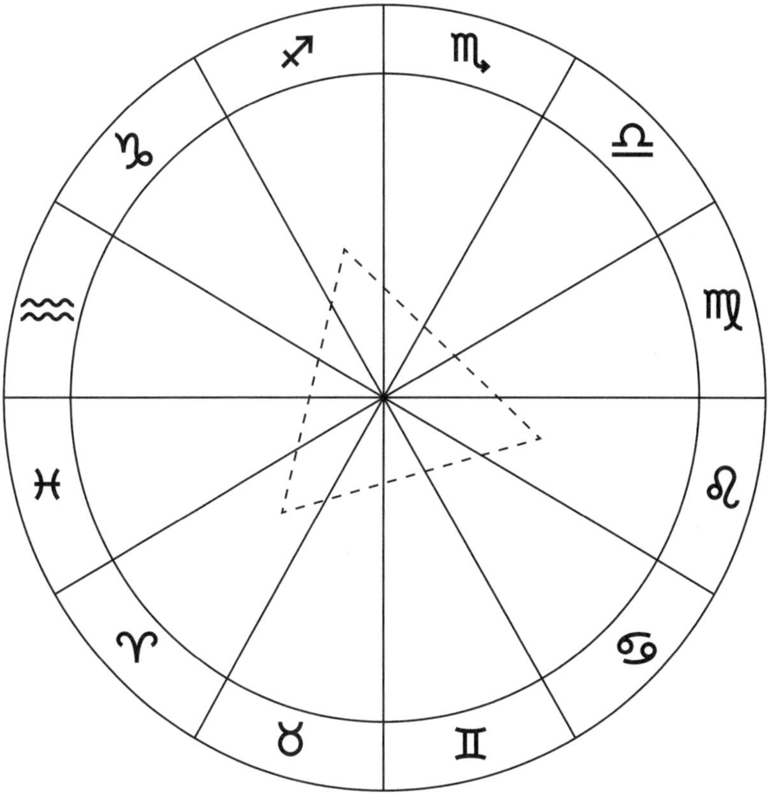

Signs of the same element trine each other. Aries, Leo, and Sagittarius are all Fire signs.

Now, check to see if your co-creator receives or makes a trine to another planet. When we're using whole-sign aspects, spotting a trine is easy. A trine aspect occurs when planets are in different zodiac signs of the same element. For example, all the Air signs trine each other, all the Fire signs trine each other, and so on.

Signs that Trine

Fire: Aries, Leo, Sagittarius

Earth: Taurus, Virgo, Capricorn

Air: Gemini, Libra, Aquarius

Water: Cancer, Scorpio, Pisces

Planets occupying signs of the same element are in similar environments. This is partly why trine aspects are considered harmonious. These planets work in the same way: They understand each other, they have access to similar tools, and they want similar things. Trines from a benefic planet, Venus or Jupiter, are golden and can boost and protect your co-creator. Trines from a malefic, Mars or Saturn, aren't as challenging as oppositions or squares, but the trine doesn't naturally erase their malefic status. There will still be some obstacles to deal with, but it's likely you can overcome them.

Sextiles

And finally, check to see if your co-creator is involved in a sextile. When using whole-sign aspects, a sextile is formed by planets in signs of the same gender or polarity (i.e., feminine signs sextile each other and masculine signs sextile each other). I think it's easiest to remember that Fire and Air signs sextile each other, and Earth and Water signs sextile each other. For example, if your natal Moon is in Taurus (Earth) and your natal Saturn is in Pisces (Water), they would create a sextile.

Signs that Sextile

Aries sextiles Gemini and Aquarius

Taurus sextiles Cancer and Pisces

Gemini sextiles Aries and Leo

Cancer sextiles Taurus and Virgo

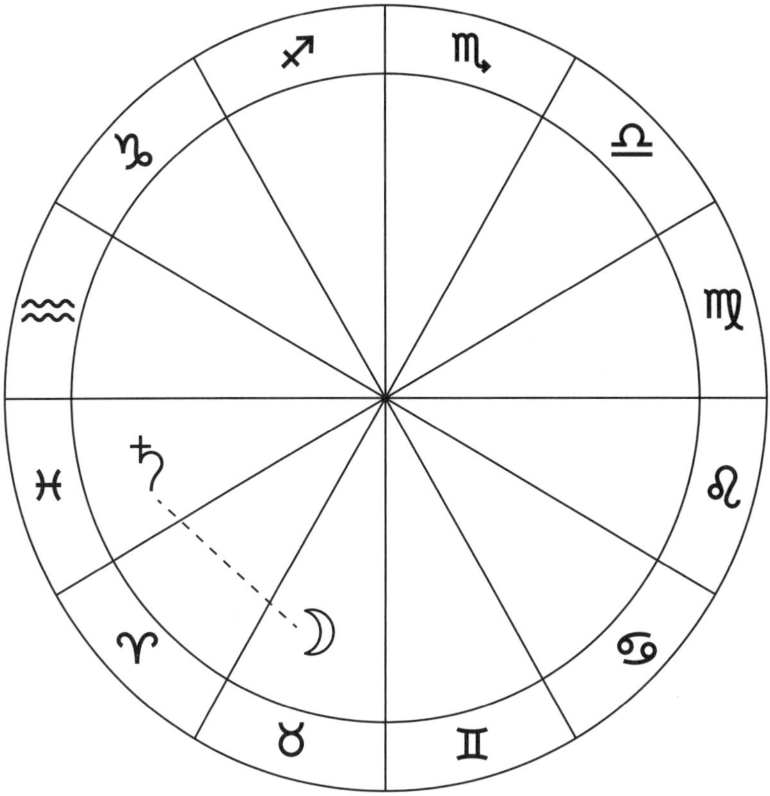

The Moon in Taurus sextiles Saturn in Pisces.

Leo sextiles Gemini and Libra

Virgo sextiles Cancer and Scorpio

Libra sextiles Leo and Sagittarius

Scorpio sextiles Virgo and Capricorn

Sagittarius sextiles Libra and Aquarius

Capricorn sextiles Scorpio and Pisces

Aquarius sextiles Aries and Sagittarius

Pisces sextiles Taurus and Capricorn

Sextiles are weaker than trines, meaning they have the least amount of *oomph* on their own and require some assistance or applying yourself to materialize. Sextiles have gifts and opportunities just like trines, but they require you to reach out and grab them. This might look like taking something that you have an aptitude for and actively working toward making it a reliable skill. Broken-record moment: Sextiles from a malefic planet, Mars or Saturn, may bring some slight irritation, while sextiles from a benefic planet, Venus or Jupiter, tend to strengthen and protect your co-creator.

It's likely that your co-creator receives a mix of celestial support or challenge. This is just like life, right? There may be some years you remember as purely "awful" or "wonderful," but for the most part, life brings a mixed bag of experiences.

What about aspects from the Sun, Moon, and Mercury? You're welcome to include aspects from these three planets in your assessment, too, but they aren't going to be as vital as the ones I described above. Remember that Mercury is an in-between planet and doesn't have a definitive benefic or malefic status, and the Sun and Moon generally function as benefics, unless the Sun causes your co-creator to be invisible, which we discussed in the Appearance section.

Take a moment to fill out the final prompt below. Repeat the prompt for each important aspect.

[Planet] makes an aspect with [Saturn/Mars/Jupiter/ Venus]. This planet is a [malefic/benefic] and brings my co-creator celestial [challenge/support].

Example: Mercury makes an aspect with Saturn. This planet is a malefic and brings my co-creator celestial challenge.

Recap

Whew! That was a lot. Well done. So, that's the CLEAR method. Now you have a checklist you can use to assess your co-creator and determine the quality and feel of your year ahead. If you've filled out the prompts, you should have a pretty lengthy paragraph describing your co-creator's condition, a.k.a. job performance. I've put them all below for easy reference. I encourage you to take it even further and rewrite this paragraph in your own words.

• • • • • • •

Prompts

[Planet]'s innate jobs are to [jobs]. In my life, [planet] also manages [house topics based on sign rulership].

I have a [day/night] chart. My co-creator [planet] is in the [day/night] club. This is a [match/mismatch].

My co-creator [planet] is [a benefic/a malefic/common/a luminary]. It's naturally [life-affirming/life-stifling], but there's always nuance to this.

My co-creator is in the sign of [zodiac sign here]. This is a [masculine/feminine] sign, which means my co-creator is more likely to be [extroverted/introverted, active/passive] and [fast/slow].

My co-creator is in a [cardinal/fixed/mutable] sign. This means that it does its job in a [forceful, steady, meandering] way.

My co-creator is in an extreme position. It's in the sign of its [rulership/detriment/exaltation/fall]. This may [enhance/inhibit] its job performance. (*Does not apply to everyone.*)

My co-creator is located in the [house number] house. [Planet] must use the topic(s) of [house topics] to express itself and do its work. This house is [angular/succedent/cadent] and considered to be a [strong/average/weak] place. This house is [bright/shady] and brings outcomes that are more [visible/invisible] and [worldly/spiritual].

My co-creator is moving [fast/slow] and is more likely to do its work [quickly/gradually].

[Planet] is [direct/retrograde/stationary], which means things this year are likely to proceed [as expected/with delays].

My co-creator is [visible/invisible] and is likely to do its work in [public/private].

[Planet] makes an aspect with [Saturn/Mars/Jupiter/Venus]. This planet is a [malefic/benefic] and brings my co-creator celestial [challenge/support].

• • • • • • •

four

How to Planet Channel

We've covered a lot of astrological theory so far! If your brain hurts, I get it. It's important to have a solid foundation in the mechanics, but I think it's equally important to bring in your intuition. It's one thing to know what astrology means on paper, but it's another to have an embodied, personal experience of it. I want to leave room for your own astrological opinions and felt-sense to form. So, let's take a detour from the theory and learn two ways of getting cosmic insight that don't require a high level of astrological know-how or skill. One I call planet channeling, and the other, planetary prayer. You're going to see both sprinkled throughout the rest of the book.

Planet Channeling

Planet channeling is a journaling technique that I naturally started doing many years ago. If we want to be technical, it's automatic writing with a splash of stream-of-consciousness, a hefty side of personal reflection, and a sprinkle of creative writing. I prefer to just say journaling. Side note: You don't need to identify as a *writer* to do this practice. This is journaling; it's for everyone.

Planet channeling is exactly what it sounds like. You give your pen over to a planet and allow it to write through you. If that sounds a little scary, don't worry. You're not leaving your body or surrendering your power. You're just inviting a planet to sit down with you for a chat and capturing what it has to say on the page.

Who are you really channeling though? I like to believe that the planets represent parts of me, especially parts of me that I may have trouble relating to or accepting. Speaking with the planets gives these estranged parts airtime. I also frequently imagine a planet as an older, wiser me. Maybe you want to imagine the planets as your ancestors, guiding you along the path, or perhaps you just settle on massive collections of energy that you can wield. Some people like to view the planets as gods and goddesses—a practice as old as time. Others, like me, who grew up in a religious environment, may feel uncomfortable with that at first. A little trick I used in the early days was to view the planets as fingers of God, busy doing God's work. These days, I use a mix of all of these perspectives in my planet channeling practice. Choose what resonates with you.

Now that you know whom you're talking to, here's how to planet channel. First, I want to be clear that I'm talking about old-school handwriting. Although you may eventually end up channeling through a keyboard or your voice, please start with plain old writing. Handwriting slows you down, eliminates excess noise, and puts you in another headspace.

My second suggestion: Get yourself a cheap notebook. This process can be messy, and I encourage you to make room for that. There's something about a new hardcover journal that gets me all pent up in my Virgo perfectionist brain. But a one-dollar notebook from the grocery store? I don't care how I "mess" that up. Trashy notebooks have power. Something about them opens the floodgates and just gives you permission to go. Also, choose a writing utensil that's smooth and allows your hand to move quickly and easily across the page. We want to foster a feeling of flow.

And then, invite a planet to have a conversation with you. It doesn't need to be formal or spiritual. Allow it to be casual and irreverent. I've been known to start with, *Hey, Saturn. What's up?* Put aside everything you know about astrology. Put aside any judgment about what may be "right" or "wrong," astrologically speaking. Allow whatever comes up to come up. Do whatever you need to do to come to the page completely raw and unfiltered. Nobody is going to read this. There's no need to be poetic. There's no need to think at all. Allow yourself to write with abandon and just let the words out.

When first starting it can be helpful to imagine the planet as a person. I like to pretend the planets are friends or even assistants who can't wait to chat with me. Dress the planet up. What's it wearing? What does it look like? What about accessories? Where does it live, and what does that space look like? What's its favorite song? Allow your creative mind to take over. Begin by writing down these fun details.

Then, just like you would with a person, start with a little small talk. *Hey, how's your day going? Can I get you something to drink?* What does this planet like to drink? How does their voice sound? What type of energy do they carry? What's the vibe when they walk into the room? I also encourage you to lift the concept of gender off the planets for this activity. Allow them to show up in whatever form they choose. For example, Venus is typically considered feminine in expression, but maybe that's not how Venus shows up today. Great. Just go with that.

And then, start capturing the conversation. This might look like a letter written to you from a planet's perspective, or my favorite, a script where you and the planet are having a dialogue. If you ever get stuck, just go back to describing what the planet would look like if it were a person. (Or an animal! Anything goes.)

When you're finished, it's a nice touch to show some gratitude. Thank the planet for spending time with you and for any insight it shared and let it know you'll be back to connect again later. Then, let your writing sit for a bit—maybe just a few minutes or overnight if you can wait. And finally, reread and apply any insight to your life.

You can channel any planet you like, but for starters, I suggest channeling your co-creator. I've given lots of prompts and opportunities to do this within each co-creator's chapter coming up, but let's have a go at it right now. Remember, this is your bestie for the year. You two are going to be close. Think of this as meeting a new friend for the first time. You're curious. You want to know everything about this person—the basics, like where they're from and what they do, but also what inspires them, what they dream about, and what motivates them.

After an easy greeting (*Hi, [planet]. I'm so excited to meet you!*), take some time to write out the details of your co-creator's appearance and the imaginary place you're meeting them. Then, ease into asking it a few questions. You can ask your co-creator anything you want, but since this may be your first time planet channeling, I've given you a few prompts below to play with. Just write out the prompt and let the planet respond.

Where are you steering me?

What's on your to-do list?

How can I work with you more effectively?

What's the number one tip you have for me?

How can I empower you?

What is it you want me to know this year?

The last question is extremely open-ended. Allow the planet to go whichever way it wants. It may have a special message for you or maybe some encouragement or very specific instructions. (I've been known to receive a ten-step plan from a planet.) Or you may just receive a feeling. Write down the sensations that come along with that feeling. It's all relevant.

Good job! First planet channeling session in the books. This will become more natural the more you do it. I encourage you to check in with your co-creator regularly. Keep in mind that your co-creator's appearance and tone of voice may change each time you check in.

That's okay and nothing to worry about. You can't do this process wrong. Trust yourself.

Planetary Prayer

Okay, I admit that planetary prayer sounds a little strange, but since you're already planet channeling, you might as well take the leap. This is another practice that started happening in my life organically, and I find it to be a powerful recentering tool. Instead of having a long conversation with a planet, planetary prayer is like shooting it a quick text. It's like asking a friend to remind you of the truth during a tough time or letting someone know you appreciate them with a heart emoji. It's a quick, accessible way to both ground yourself and ask for divine intervention.

Although you'll find a planetary "prayer" in each of the planet chapters, please rename it whatever you want. Maybe the word *prayer* makes you feel icky. That's cool; use *mantra, intention,* or *reminder* instead. And even though the prayers are addressed to a planet, you can direct them to whomever you want. Just like in planet channeling, you get to choose who you're talking to. Maybe you direct the prayer to a benevolent force outside of yourself, or perhaps you direct the prayer inward as a conjuring of your most authentic self.

I use the prayers sporadically and casually throughout the day. I might mutter one under my breath in the grocery store or write one out a few times in my journal as a more intentional practice. Carry them with you on notecards, make them the background of your phone—they're meant to be taken on the go.

Feel free to make up your own prayers too. If you do, I suggest using present tense, as if the benefit or outcome is already here. For example, I may feel very out of my own flow, but using the prayer, "Thank you, Moon, for showing me how to live in my flow" acts as a statement of belief that even if I don't feel in flow right now, it *is* possible.

five

A Primer on Transits

At this point you're probably itching to flip to the second half of the book and read as much as you can about your co-creator and house of the year. But before you do that, I have one last piece of theory to teach you.

Recap: Annual profections are the big brushstrokes. They identify the general content and quality of the year. They also identify your co-creator planet. But *when* are these main events likely to take place? And what about other storylines not caught by profections? Enter transits. This is an oversimplification, but here goes: Profections tell you *what*. Transits tell you *when*.

Transits are probably the most popular timing technique in astrology today. Transits are a ridiculously massive topic that one could write multiple books about. Here, I'm going to explain the essentials so that you can start understanding transits ASAP. I describe each transit in detail within the co-creator chapters. To watch transits closely, you'll need your favorite astrology app, software, or a personalized astrology almanac (my preference). Check the "Resources" in the back of the book for my suggestions.

The word *transit* implies travel. In astrology, it refers to a planet in today's sky "walking around" your birth chart and coming into contact with one of your natal planets either by snuggling up next to it or by staring at it from somewhere across the cosmic room. A transit involves at least two players: the natal planet being activated or receiving the transit and the planet doing the activating or transiting. For example, real-time Saturn may walk around your chart and relate to your natal Moon. Or real-time Venus may walk around your chart and relate to your natal Venus. Transits may show up as an event, change, opportunity, challenge, lesson, transition, or person. Basically, transits describe the motion of life. They're astrological descriptions of what's happening right now.

Similar to profections but slightly different, transits activate certain parts of your birth chart and make them operational. Transits act as timing triggers. Something from the outside (the planet in the real-time sky, which I'll call the *transiting planet* from now on) interacts with a part of your life (what I'll call the *natal planet*). When a major transit turns on a specific part of your chart, you get a master class in how that part of you or your life works. Let's pretend your natal Mercury is receiving a transit. Well, whatever your natal Mercury represents is being turned on or emphasized. This includes its job and its potential or ability to do its job well. Since we've already gone through this in detail, I won't repeat it here. To discover what a certain natal planet means, take it through the CLEAR method in chapter three.

Let's pause for a sovereign astrology mindset moment. You don't get to choose your transits, and I personally don't believe you can 100 percent control how they show up—let's be real, unexpected things happen—but you do get to choose how you respond to them. Instead of thinking about what a transit is going to "do to you," try asking, *What do I want to do with it?* I encourage you not to think about transits as making you do something or making you feel something but simply as external information that requires a response after some processing. You get to choose how a transit informs your decisions.

It's also good to know that transits may have a moment of exactness, but that doesn't mean an event will occur at that exact time. In my experience, events correlated with a transit may occur anywhere from a couple of days before to a couple of days after the exact transit. Depending on the transit, it may be an even longer window. So when you're watching transits, don't just limit yourself to the exact day—broaden your horizons.

Also keep in mind that sometimes a transit's outcome or meaning may not be perceptible to you just yet. I like to think of this as a transit working for you behind the scenes. For example, you may be having a delightful transit from Jupiter and not notice anything going on, only to be told a few weeks later that something to your benefit really did happen around that time—you just didn't know about it. I like to trust the transits. I like to believe that goodness is happening for me behind the scenes.

Prioritizing Transits

The problem with transits is that there are so many of them. You're having multiple transits per day, most days, and trying to pay attention to all is astrology TMI and not something I would recommend. For the most part, you won't notice anything significant—maybe just a passing mood at most. But then sometimes a transit will come around and something really significant will happen. You get that promotion, you receive extremely important news, or you finally make a decision about something that's been weighing on you. How do you know which transits will amount to something and which won't? Profections.

Now that you've mastered profections, you're ready to layer in transits. Profections act like a prioritization system for transits, telling you which ones to pay attention to and which ones to ignore. Not all transits are created equal. Below is a brief rundown of what to pay attention to. We'll go into each one in detail in the sections that follow.

Transits that Matter

Transits to your natal co-creator

Transits from your transiting co-creator

Transits through your house and sign of the year

Sign and direction changes of your transiting co-creator

And . . . voilà! See what just happened? Just like that, hundreds of meaningless transits just went out the window. Sweet relief. Now, there are some outliers, of course, but just start with these. These transits are the ones most likely to correlate with the main events of your year.

Transits to Your Natal Co-Creator

Your natal co-creator is somewhere in the zodiac, and planets in today's sky can come around and turn it on by transit. For example, let's pretend your co-creator is Venus, and your Venus is in Gemini in the eleventh house. Maybe Jupiter comes to Gemini in the eleventh house and activates your Venus by conjunction (nice!), or maybe Mars comes to Sagittarius in the fifth house and opposes your natal Venus (mixed bag!). These are both examples of transits. Any transit to your natal co-creator can be important, but you can prioritize them even further. In my experience, transits to your natal co-creator from the superior planets (i.e., slower planets with orbits outside of the earth's orbit)—Mars, Jupiter, Saturn, Uranus, Neptune, and Pluto—are the most significant. I would also throw an eclipse into the significant pile.

Transits from Your Transiting Co-Creator

Your co-creator is also a planet moving around in the sky right now. You're now having a masterclass on this planet. You two are a team, remember? You want to know everything you can about this planet, including where it is in the sky right now. Keep tabs on it. Really. As your co-creator moves around the sky, it's going to come into contact with other planets in your natal chart. Let's use our same Venus example. Let's pretend today's transiting Venus is in Taurus. What if you have the Moon there? Well, that's a transit that you'll want to pay attention to. Prioritize transits from your transiting co-creator to your visible natal planets (Sun, Moon, Mercury, Venus, Mars, Jupiter, and Saturn). In my experience, transits to your natal outer planets (Uranus, Neptune, Pluto) aren't very noticeable.

Transits Through Your House and Sign of the Year

Remember too that your house of the year has all the lights turned on. It's the part of your chart that's the real focal point this year. So, if that house welcomes a new guest (a.k.a. a transiting planet moving through), you're going to want to pay attention. Take special note if there's a retrograde cycle or an eclipse happening in your house/sign of the year. You'll probably feel this more than usual.

Sign and Direction Changes of Your Transiting Co-Creator

You also want to know about anything your co-creator planet is doing in the sky right now. You want to know what sign it's in. You want to know if it's traveling retrograde or direct. You want to know if it's in a powerful place or struggling a little bit. After watching profections and transits for over a decade now, I've noticed that major turning points tend to unfold when the co-creator switches directions. For example, the day my co-creator stationed direct (began moving forward again), I was approached about writing this book. Pretty cool, huh?

More Transits, Please!

If you still have some brain space and you want some more, well, there are always more transits to track. I highly recommend capping it at your co-creator, but let's be honest, there are some other movers and shakers out there. My suggestion is to pay attention to transits from the superior, slower-moving planets to visible planets and angles in your natal chart. Again, the superior planets are Mars, Jupiter, Saturn, Uranus, Neptune, and Pluto.

And finally, the transits that may be the most noticeable are the more dynamic aspects: the conjunction, square, and opposition. Now, I don't want to discount trines and sextiles. Of course they're important too. But when you're first starting out, you may want to simplify your transit list even further by paying attention to the more "tense" aspects. I don't mean tense in a bad way; I mean that these aspects tend to create action and outcomes, which is usually easier to spot in an objective sense.

six

Your House of the Year

You've made it through the theory! Now that you know your co-creator and house of the year, it's time to learn as much as you can about them. In this section, you'll find everything you need to know about the topics of your house of the year. Be sure to answer the reflection questions so that you can personalize the information and make the most of it. After you've read about your house of the year, find your co-creator planet's section and explore what layers of meaning it has to add to the story.

First House: Rising, Hour Marker, Helm, Ascendant

Angular, Favorable

Ages: 0, 12, 24, 36, 48, 60, 72, 84, 96

Topics: Life direction, vitality, body, health, wellness, constitution, character, personality, first impressions, appearance, self-expression, beginnings

When you advance into a first-house year, you kick off a new twelve-year cycle. It's associated with beginnings, starting fresh, and stepping out. Each time you come to the first house, it's like being reborn. First-house years, similar to twelfth-house years, are a time of transition. But instead of things coming to a close, you've moved through the dark night and are emerging into the dawn. This is a transition from endings to beginnings, from darkness to light, from stillness to motion, and from invisibility to visibility.

The first house is arguably one of the most important in your chart and represents your life, your body, your personality, and all that makes you "you." When your first house is highlighted, general life direction tends to become the main focus. You may notice, especially in hindsight, that this year puts you on a new path for the next twelve. The decisions you make and the steps you take this year set up your trajectory for the next decade plus.

Ancient astrologers often used the analogy of a ship to describe the chart. The first house was called the helm, which is the wheel that steers the ship. This is a house about direction, and advancing into this house is like your ship setting sail. There may be a long way to go, but the bags are packed and the map is out. This is a time of focusing on what you want for your life and steering your ship in that direction.

I view first-house times as steps of faith. You may not fully know where you're going yet, but when you take one step, the next step is made clear. As you take action, the path opens up and so does your vision and perspective. Keep tweaking your route as new information and clarity come in and learn to rely on your inner compass.

First-house years are also about the vessel that carries you through life—your body. When you enter a first-house year, it's very common for your attention and focus to turn to your physical body and how you care for it. I've seen people begin new wellness routines during these years, have a health wake-up call, change their style and appearance, or just focus on finding a sense of balance.

• • • • • • •

From My Case Files

Susi moved across the country and explored self-expression while writing a book on the intersection of myth, astrology, and her family history.

Emma took practical steps toward a new professional direction in end-of-life care and soul midwifery.

From My Journals

During my most recent first-house year, my first book, *Body Astrology*, was published and set me up for the pattern of writing astrology books for, I hope, the next twelve years or more.

Reflection Questions

What themes am I ready to leave behind?

What themes would I like to develop over the next twelve years?

I'm packing a bag for the next twelve years—what's in it?

If I could take my life anywhere or do anything—with no excuses and no holding back—where and what would it be?

Although it may be subtle or obvious, what's the first step?

Make a first-house time capsule that captures the basic facts: Where are you living? Where are you working? What's your day-to-day life like?

• • • • • • •

Second House: Gate of Hades

Succedent, Unfavorable

Ages: 1, 13, 25, 37, 49, 61, 73, 85, 97

Topics: Money, livelihood, income, revenue, cash flow, resources (tangible and intangible), possessions, spending habits, saving habits, budgets, self-worth, values

In the first-house year, you determined the vision: where you're going and what the next twelve years will be about. In the second-house year, you begin gathering and cultivating the resources necessary to make that vision manifest.

One of the main topics that the ancient astrologers gave to the second house was livelihood: how you support your life by providing the necessities like food, shelter, and money, to name a few. This meaning is still relevant today. The second house is often just considered the money house, but I like to broaden its meaning to include anything that you use to build up and fortify your life. Yes, it's a place of money, but in my opinion, it's also a place of possessions, skills, and time. When you enter a second-house year, you enter a season of relating to these resources in a deeper way and perhaps reshaping how they flow in and out of your life.

A second-house year gives you an opportunity to evaluate how your resources are gathered. It's natural to question the paths through which money comes to you, whether that's a job, a career, a partner, or something else. If you're currently working, you may experience a change in pay or simply begin to wonder if your current job supports you on more levels than just a paycheck. You might also question the relationship between time and money and explore how you can separate the two.

If the astrological circumstances surrounding the second house are challenging, these times may be less about what you want to do and more about making ends meet. On the other hand, when astrological circumstances are favorable, second-house times can be very lucrative.

But a second-house year isn't just about how you bring resources in, it's about how you spend them. Whether it's by choice or necessity, reworking budgets and spending and saving habits tend to come with a second-house year. I encourage you to take a proactive approach and educate yourself on finance. Don't forget to assess how you spend your "intangible" resources like time and energy too.

• • • • • • •

From My Case Files

Bri spent her second-house resources opening a production house that specializes in esoteric productions. She secured the company's first investor and thought a lot about her relationship with money, her definition of success, and how she could use these things to help her community thrive.

Angela spent a lot of time thinking and writing about what she values and what her "value" is. When asked what's taken most of her time and attention this year, she answered, "A lot of writing about understanding performative or transactional relationships where I'm always and only the giver and what's my 'value' if I'm not giving."

From My Journals

As a young teen, my second-house year was spent babysitting so I could save up for a camera. Later, I started grad school, which coincided with taking on student loans (a second- and eighth-house thing). And in my most recent second-house cycle, I received a royalty check for my first book.

Reflection Questions

What's my personal definition of wealth?

What was I taught about money growing up? How does this inform my money story today?

If I say yes to this, what am I saying no to?

Am I spending my "capital" (money, time, energy, brainpower) in a way that feels good to me?

What makes me feel supported and how can I cultivate more of this?

• • • • • • •

Third House: Goddess

Cadent, Semi-favorable

Ages: 2, 14, 26, 38, 50, 62, 74, 86, 98

Topics: Siblings, relatives, neighbors, local community, short-distance travel and journeys, communication, writing, daily spiritual practice, ritual, early education, trainings and courses, media, marketing

When you enter a third-house year, a myriad of themes can pop up. This house covers a lot of ground and includes everything from daily spiritual practice to communication, learning, relatives, neighbors, and short-distance travel.

The third house is called Goddess. As the name suggests, this house and its partner across the wheel, called God, are the in-between spaces in the chart where the veil between the seen world and the spirit world is a little thinner. Communication, travel, knowledge, and spirituality were intimately tied in the ancient world. A ninth-house pilgrimage may take a year, but a third-house ritual may just require a walk to town. What else required a walk to town? Exchanging knowledge and exchanging goods. This is where not only short journeys and communication enter the third house but also commerce. In my mind, the third house is where hot gossip is exchanged over a hot drink. Emails, texts, phone calls, and meetings over coffee are all third-house modes of communication.

The third house oversees everything from speaking to writing, and when it's activated by profection, you might find yourself spending a lot of time doing these things in a learning environment, a working environment, or for fun. Third-house years can help you develop your communication style as well as understand your communication needs, especially in the context of relationships with neighbors and relatives. Social media is another third-house arena, and there may be increased sharing or visibility in this sector when you enter a third-house year.

Sometimes, third-house years are less about you directly and more about the people around you. For example, the third house traditionally rules siblings, and third-house years can either highlight your relationship with them and/or bring about events in their lives. For example, maybe a sibling has a child, gets married, or goes through a hard time.

Neighbors are another group of people the third house represents. Third-house years might be spent having a great time with neighbors turned friends or the opposite—when those relationships sour and become awkward or strained. Neighbors can also be expanded to include your community, and you may notice a desire, whether online or in person, to get involved and make connections.

• • • • • • •

From My Case Files

Hilda, who grew up wanting to be a writer, started working on her book proposal again after taking a break. She spent time researching and reading comparative titles and hopes to find an agent.

Hollie had multiple incidents of terrible car trouble (the third house rules transportation) and navigated a relationship with a neighbor that took an awkward turn.

From My Journals

As a teen, my third-house year free time was spent making my first website and obsessing over whether my friends were going to email me back. Another third-house year was spent at school (a third-house place), where I met and started dating my husband.

Reflection Questions

What conversations am I interested in having or hosting?

What type and frequency of communication works for me? What doesn't?

Is there a form of communication that I'd like to develop or nurture?

What would I like to learn? How can I learn it in an easy, close-to-home way?

Who do I want to gather with? Where are they and what are they talking about?

How can simple sacredness be woven into my life?

• • • • • • •

Fourth House: Subterranean

Angular, Favorable

Ages: 3, 15, 27, 39, 51, 63, 75, 87, 99

Topics: Parents, father, home, ancestors, roots, foundations, history, hidden things, the end of things, real estate, land

Subterranean means "below the surface of the earth," which gives rise to the idea of foundations. The fourth house is your roots, where and whom you come from. This is the house of parents, particularly the father in the ancient model, as well as the family home or land. This is a very earthy house that rules real estate and other things that were, at least in older times, thought to anchor one's status into place.

Today, the fourth house still represents your parents but also the home you currently live in and sometimes those you live with. When the fourth house is highlighted, home life becomes the focus. It can be about an actual brick-and-mortar home or the people who are home for you. Sometimes moving or buying and selling real estate, remodeling, or signing or breaking a lease occurs during these times. Sometimes professional pursuits take a back seat to family matters, like aging parents or other things going on behind closed doors at home.

I consider the fourth house as representing the support in your life, mostly tangible but also intangible. It's the foundation that your life is built upon. Some of us have charts with very sturdy foundations, and some of us have charts with more mutable foundations, but we all have a fourth house. Depending on the astrological context, during a fourth-house period, you may be building up your foundation or letting go of things that you once thought secure. This is a great time to cultivate an unseen, internal stability—in other words, a deep sense that you have your own back no matter how things shift externally.

In practice, a subtler theme I've noticed come up during fourth-house years is boundary setting. Boundaries are another type of foundation or limit that ground us and create a sense of safety and security. Fourth-house seasons might include creating these boundaries for the first time or the harder work of asserting (and reasserting) them with the people in your life.

When something is subterranean, it's also hidden, underground, and this is where some of the ancient fourth-house associations with death, graves, secrets, and endings come from. This is arguably one of the most private pieces of your chart.

• • • • • • •

From My Case Files

Steph moved twice!

Susheela spent most of her time studying astrology in the basement (the fourth house rules basements) in preparation to open her own practice.

From My Journals

Out of the four fourth-house years I've lived through so far, three of them contained a major move, and two of those moves were overseas. My grandfather passed away during one of these years, and my most recent fourth-house year began with me living in a three-generation household.

Reflection Questions

What makes me feel externally anchored and secure?

What makes me feel internally anchored and secure?

If everything were washed away, what would be at the foundation of my life?

How can I ensure that what I'm building now is made to last?

How can I feel more supported in my home life?

Where and who do I come from, and how does that inform my life today?

• • • • • • •

Fifth House: Good Fortune

Succedent, Favorable

Ages: 4, 16, 28, 40, 52, 64, 76, 88, 100

Topics: Children, sexuality and reproduction, creativity, the arts, pleasure and leisure, gifts, good luck

The fifth house is called Good Fortune, and as the name suggests, many of life's joys are represented by this house. The traditional meaning of this house is children. Yes, children as bringers of joy, but especially in the ancient world, children as actual bearers of fortune—they would be expected to carry on the family business, care for you when you're old, or marry into fortune and share that fortune with you. During a fifth-house year, if they're a part of your life, children and parenting may become a more central focus.

The fifth house and the first house are connected by a trine, the most positive relationship in astrology, which is where this house gets some of its good vibes. Regardless of the presence of physical children, the fifth house keeps the life of your first house going. In other words, fifth-house things are pathways you use to multiply yourself. They're ways your life force bears "fruit." How do you replicate yourself in miniature? When we put children aside, this is creativity. The fifth house is the place of art, dance, performance, and anything else you can distill your life force into. But also think about the swelling emotion and pleasure that comes from enjoying a great movie or concert—that's fifth house too. Fifth-house times are about making space for enjoyment, whether you find that at the dance studio or the tennis court.

Romance and sexuality belong to the fifth house too, and fifth-house years may nudge you to explore these themes more deeply. No, there's no guarantee that you'll fall in love during a fifth-house year, but the desire for intimate connection and fulfilling partnership is definitely there, as well as the need to express your sexuality more fully. Fifth-house years also commonly bring up themes of reproductive health and rights.

The fifth house also carries the theme of receiving gifts. Think about the three wise men (who were astrologers, I might add). Did they come empty-handed to visit baby Jesus? No. They brought gold, frankincense, and myrrh. Back in the day, ambassadors and emissaries always brought gifts, hoping it would increase their favor with whatever leader they were meeting. When you advance into the fifth house, you may be on the receiving end of this good fortune, so be on the lookout.

• • • • • • •

From My Case Files

Ashley embraced the "single-girl life" and had the deep realization that she didn't need an intimate partner or kids to have family.

Aminta began identifying as Queer, and when asked to sum up the past year in a single phrase said, "Becoming more of myself."

From My Journals

As a teenager, I fell in love for the first time during a fifth-house year. I was living abroad and reconnected with an old friend from middle school and sparks flew. We would meet up in beautiful European cities and explore—what a fortune!

Reflection Questions

What is my "art"? What do I generate with my life force, and how can I make more space for it?

How can I make this [job/project/business/fill in the blank] feel like art?

Where can I insert more fun and leisure into my schedule?

What would delight me this year?

How can I support my [creative/physical] children?

• • • • • • •

Sixth House: Bad Fortune

Cadent, Unfavorable

Ages: 5, 17, 29, 41, 53, 65, 77, 89

Topics: Illness, accidents, injury, work, employers, employees, co-workers, service, military, pets, routine, bad luck

I know the bluntness of the old term *bad fortune* is intense, but before you freak out, I want to gently remind you that you've probably already experienced a vast array of good fortune and bad fortune in your life. Suffering is a part of the human experience and traditional astrology simply doesn't shy away from that. It doesn't brush suffering under the rug, and because of that, I view it as very kind. In the right hands, it acknowledges and addresses the reality of life instead of denying it, which usually makes people feel unheard and unseen.

The word *fortune* speaks more about the physical realm—like body, wealth, possessions, and so on—while the word *spirit* (as in the twelfth house "Bad Spirit") speaks more about the intangible realm. The sixth house of Bad Fortune tends to represent the more physical side of suffering in life, like illness and injury, enemies, a crappy job, or just plain bad luck.

In ancient times, the sixth house included slavery, servitude, and other forms of oppression. It's important to remember that slavery still exists today, through human trafficking, child labor, and other conditions where people are exploited. But these sixth-house themes have largely been watered down for the average astrological audience to work, employment, and service jobs. And although I agree and have seen this ring true in practice, it's important to remember where these themes originated.

Daily routine and rituals have also made their way into the sixth house. This is probably because, for most people, their job defines the order of their day, including what time they wake up, when they shower, what they wear, when and where they eat, and other mundane details of daily life. Health has also been lumped into the sixth house, but I really want to make sure you understand that the first house is where good health resides, and the sixth house is where things that thwart good health reside.

When your sixth house is activated, first of all, like I've said before, I don't want you entering that time expecting misfortune. But I do think it's wise to use it as a reminder to think about how you deal with challenging times if and when they pop up. As with everything in the human experience, sixth-house times are a mixed bag. They may or may not be in-your-face awful, but they could feel grinding or labor intensive, where your schedule is packed with back-to-back classes, meetings, shifts, obligations, or anything else that takes a pattern of sleep, eat, get on the hamster wheel again. We all go through periods like that.

• • • • • • • •

From My Case Files

Izzy described the year as a "turning point." It was a mixed bag of going through a very difficult breakup, getting promoted at work, and spending a lot of time with practitioners focusing on trauma healing.

When asked to sum up the year in one phrase, Cristina said, "Working toward sustainability." She spent a lot of time focusing on her day-to-day experience and figuring out a schedule that was livable, balanced, and met her own needs as well as those of her husband and son.

From My Journals

My father was deployed during my first sixth-house year. (The sixth house also represents the military.) In a later sixth-house year, I found myself extremely busy juggling work, getting two master's degrees, and managing mysterious chronic pain—you could say I wasn't loving life at that time.

Reflection Questions

How do I care for myself during a challenging day, week, or month? (Write these things out as a list that you can read when things are tough. For example, a list of things that make me smile, a list of things that remind me the world is bigger than my problems, etc.)

How can I support my body as it carries me through challenging or demanding times?

What routine tweaks would create more flow and comfort in my day?

What's most essential right now? Can I give myself permission to do that and nothing more?

What are my limits with this? How do I know when enough is enough?

Is this tough or toxic?

• • • • • • •

Seventh House: Setting, Descendant

Angular, Favorable

Ages: 6, 18, 30, 42, 54, 66, 78, 90

Topics: Marriage, spouses, intimate relationships, personal and business partnerships, the other party in a business deal or negotiation, clients, and patients

The first house is where the Sun rises; the seventh house is where the Sun sets. The zodiac sign that occupies your seventh house was the one descending below the horizon when you were born, which is where a common name for this area of the chart, the descendant, comes from.

If the first house is all about you, its opposite, the seventh house, is all about them—the other, the not you. The main traditional meaning of this house is spouse or marriage, but we can broaden this to include any other partnership that's bound by some type of contract or agreement. These aren't casual relationships but more intimate or professional partnerships that have a set container. When the seventh house is activated, relationships are the main dish, and all other-focused themes take precedence. In work, this may include a focus on your clientele, customers, buyers, or community, and their experience with what you offer.

Seventh-house times may also highlight themes of collaboration and working with others, which can bring a new dimension and maturity to what you do. Compromise and negotiation are big seventh-house topics too. And because it involves people, it's only natural that it brings a little conflict and competition as well. This house always represents the other party in a business deal, legal matter, or professional relationship.

In my research, I've also noticed many clients either start businesses or experience increased business success during seventh-house years. This puzzled me at first, but then I was reminded that a business, although we tend to think of it as an extension of ourselves, is actually another entity that we have a deep relationship or "contract" with—definitely a seventh-house thing.

Because it's an angular house, seventh-house-year events tend to be pivotal. They're the things that you really remember, that turn the wheel of your life.

• • • • • • •

From My Case Files

Most of Bonnie's attention was focused on helping her husband through a challenging mental health season. She also spent a lot of time holding space for others who were sometimes quite literally under attack. (I should clarify that a tricky Mars was Bonnie's co-creator, which is why these relational themes were so difficult and Mars flavored.) Bonnie had to stay mindful not to absorb the emotions of those she was working to support.

Mary spent time building an audience on Substack (the seventh house rules potential clients) and simultaneously worked on launching her art business.

From My Journals

I started college during one seventh-house year and met someone there who would impact my life forever. In a later seventh-house year, I got married and officially started my astrology business.

Reflection Questions

Do my primary relationships truly support me? How can I enrich them?

How can I be in partnership while also meeting my own needs?

How does what I do/make/offer serve others?

Who can I connect or collaborate with? Who can I ask for help?

What would really turn the wheel of my life this year?

• • • • • • •

Eighth House: Idle Place

Succedent, Unfavorable

Ages: 7, 19, 31, 43, 55, 67, 79, 91

Topics: Death, shared resources, gains from a spouse or partner, investments, taxes, debt, loans, inheritances, wills and trusts, change and transformation, mental illness, fear and frozenness, inactivity, grief

The ancient name for this house is the Idle Place. This is considered an inactive and passive part of the chart partly because when the Sun reaches this part of the sky each day, it's losing power and sitting low. Think about what the word *idle* means—"to pass time doing nothing," "to wait around and lollygag," "to be inactive by your own choosing," or "to be made inactive by some type of misfortune like injury, illness, or death." Yes, the eighth house is the main house of death in the chart because it's the ultimate form of idleness—but don't freak out! Advancing into an eighth-house year does not—I repeat, *does not*—mean someone will die. However, coming face-to-face with mortality and impermanence is usually an undulating theme.

There are thousands of ways to interpret the eighth house in the land of the living. For example, "idleness" as a means to financial gain or loss. As the opposing partner to the second house, the eighth house is another main money house but usually somebody else worked for this money. It governs fortunes gained or lost through death like inheritances and trusts or other forms of "idle" money like investments, loans, or money flowing to you from a partner. The idea is, you're not actively working for this money like you are in the second house.

Another way to think about the eighth house is through the lens of inactivity and things that keep you feeling frozen or like you're on the sidelines of life. One way I experience this is through the fears and anxieties that keep me from doing the things I want. The eighth house is traditionally a place of mental anguish and mental illness. When you advance into the eighth house, it's possible to come into closer contact with the things that scare you. It doesn't mean you'll be overtaken by fear; rather, you'll have an opportunity to work with it. For example, I've seen many people move into an eighth-house time ready to finally address their mental and spiritual health concerns with a professional.

Although a lot can happen beneath the surface during an eighth-house year, there might not be a lot to observe from the outside. This isn't typically a house that represents outward-facing success or climbing the ladder. Rather, its work is deep and internal. Because of this, it's a really great time to question your beliefs around work ethic, "hustle culture," and receiving. Sometimes when the eighth house is activated, you're asked to slow down or wait. This can be uncomfortable and is often oppositional to what we're told is "acceptable."

• • • • • • •

From My Case Files

When asked to describe her eighth-house year, Jessica said, "It's felt like drudging through a swamp of waiting."

Aminta focused on paying off credit card debt and experienced a few injuries that left them on the eighth-house sidelines for a few weeks.

From My Journals

So far, in all of my eighth-house years, I've benefited from another person's loss or large purchase. For example, due to the sad passing of my grandmother, my parents purchased a property with their inheritance that will eventually be passed down to me and my siblings.

Reflection Questions

What do I think about modern culture's push to go, go, go? Do I agree with it?

Where can I slow down in my life?

Where in my life is doing less the way to do more?

Where and how can accepting "idleness" create ease and permission in my life?

Where is my "idleness" due to a fear that I can compassionately address?

What fears or anxieties am I ready to look at this year? Who or what can help me with that?

• • • • • • •

Ninth House: God

Cadent, Favorable

Ages: 8, 20, 32, 44, 56, 68, 80, 92

Topics: Religion, spirituality, higher education and learning, foreign places and people, long-distance travel and journeys, language, publishing, broadcasting, divination, astrology, law, philosophy

Across the wheel from the third house, Goddess, is its partner the ninth house, God. These houses share many themes, but the context is slightly different. The ninth house is above the horizon, in the realm of day, and close to the bright and visible Midheaven (the highest part of your chart). The third house, Goddess, is below the horizon in the realm of night. Both places of the sky are otherworldly and spiritual, but unlike the closer-to-earth, more human realm of goddess spirituality, the ninth house deals in loftiness. Whether it shows up as public worship, an overseas move, a university campus, a global broadcast, or space travel, the ninth house has a big reach, and its years are often about broadening your horizons.

Ninth-house themes like travel, trade, knowledge, and spirituality were intimately tied in the ancient world. Knowledge and goods were spread by travelers and merchants. Reading and writing were often reserved for those in privileged spiritual or royal positions. And if you wanted to visit a sacred place for healing and blessing or to receive education, you usually had to travel very far away from home. When you advance into a ninth-house year, it's common for several of these themes to overlap. You may take a significant trip, enter into a serious course of study, and initiate or enrich an existing spiritual practice.

The ninth house is like a megaphone. It spreads its message far and wide. This is a place of disseminating and broadcasting information on a global scale. It's associated with publishing and media, and when you advance into a ninth-house time, you may feel the urge to get your ideas across in a significant way. This might show up as starting a blog or a podcast, teaching a workshop, or growing your social media presence.

This is also a year about gathering and giving wisdom. It's common to collect certifications and online courses like it's your full-time job. There's often an insatiable desire to learn and the feeling that you can never know enough. Topics might range from foreign language to astrology. (Yes, fun fact: This is the house of astrology.)

Speaking of wisdom, the ninth house is a place of mentors and other people you look to for guidance. You might hire a coach, seek advice from an elder, or feel inspired to act in that capacity for another. However, I'd like to offer a caution. I have quite a bit of action in my ninth house, and much of my early life involved entanglements with spiritual authority figures using their "wisdom" to manipulate me. When you're dealing with the ninth house, I think it's always important to keep in contact with your inner authority. As an astrologer who's now often in the adviser role, I'm acutely aware of when people are trying to hand me their authority. And I give it right back to them. During a ninth-house year, beware of getting stuck seeking wisdom outside of yourself or going into divination spirals where you're constantly seeking a sign out there somewhere.

• • • • • • •

From My Case Files

Caroline opened a business translating astrology texts into French. (Translation and astrology are both ruled by the ninth house.)

Jacqueline started a podcast and put the final touches on her fourth book about writing with the Moon.

From My Journals

During one of my ninth-house years, I switched majors in college several times, finally landing on business entrepreneurship. (It was my dream at the time to open a café.) In a later ninth-house year, my friend Miranda and I published *Moon Pages*, a guided Moon journal. This was my very first astrological publication.

Reflection Questions

What's the message I want to share? What's the best way to broadcast this message?

Would I benefit from more education or training?

Would I benefit from an external source of wisdom?

Would I benefit from relocation or a temporary change of scenery?

How do I know when I'm in contact with my personal authority? What does it feel like?

How do I leave space for others to have their own wisdom and authority?

How am I a conduit for Source?

Tenth House: Midheaven

Angular, Favorable

Ages: 9, 21, 33, 45, 57, 69, 81, 93

Topics: Career, public reputation, public role, recognition, honors, awards, achievements, visibility, popularity, life direction, what you're known for

The tenth house is called Midheaven, or the middle of heaven, because this is where the Sun finds its highest point during the day. This already gives us a good idea of what the tenth house is all about. During the height of the day, you can see and be seen. This house is all about visibility: what you are known for and how you are viewed. In modern day, this is often simplified to your career or profession, but it can also refer to your role in society and how you contribute.

When you advance into a tenth-house year, career and professional matters tend to take a central role. This is usually a time of ambition and achievement, and because the tenth house is angular, tenth-house years often bring pivotal life milestones. Perhaps you land your dream job, graduate from college, or become a parent. That last one may feel a bit out of place so let me explain. The tenth house also governs your roles and "titles" in society. Becoming a spouse, becoming a parent, and becoming a boss are all changes to your tenth-house status.

When the tenth house is highlighted, public image also becomes a priority. This could be about public visibility or invisibility and your comfort or discomfort with that. This could also be about perceived achievement versus failure. I'm going to be real with you: A tough activation of the tenth house can be a professional wake-up call.

When the tenth house is highlighted for someone who feels unsure about career, they tend to start inquiring about purpose and may get serious about choosing a definitive path. If the tenth house is activated for someone who's already established in a role, professional or otherwise, they may be challenged to move into an even higher level of mastery or responsibility with that role, or they may decide to put it down completely and transition to something new.

• • • • • • •

From My Case Files

Britt had several opportunities to take on new leadership roles, step into the limelight, and be more visible in her career. She also began a rebrand of her business.

Hollie spent a lot of time "rebranding" herself and networking in hopes of getting a new job. Update: She got one!

From My Journals

At age twenty-one, I graduated from college and began my entrepreneurial journey. In a later tenth-house year, my astrology career was really taking off, and I finally started to gain recognition for my work.

Reflection Questions

Where do I shine, and how can I do more of that?

What does success mean to me?

How do I feel about being visible? Through which channels am I comfortable being seen or found?

Where do I have influence, and how can I use it positively?

How have I achieved things in the past, and do I want to continue with that approach?

What's my next tenth-house milestone?

• • • • • • •

Eleventh House: Good Spirit

Succedent, Favorable

Ages: 10, 22, 34, 46, 58, 70, 82, 94

Topics: Friends, groups, associations (professional or otherwise), community, alliances, hopes, wishes, dreams, goals, prosperity, faith

Across the wheel from the fifth house, Good Fortune, is its partner the eleventh house, called Good Spirit. The common denominator here is the word *good*, but what's the difference between fortune and spirit? When we're talking about fortune, we're usually talking about prosperity that we can see and touch. When we're talking about spirit, we're usually talking about intangible benefits, though they may have very tangible outcomes. Good Spirit takes the glass-half-full approach. It's the place of hope, faith, optimism, morale, belief, and goodwill. Whether you want to call it the Universe, the Holy Spirit, your fairy godmother, your guides, a mentor, or a friend, Good Spirit encourages outside forces and people to act on your behalf.

When your eleventh house is activated, it's time to get reacquainted with the good spirit within you. This is an opportunity to reconnect with your dreams and hopes, to consciously develop or repair your faith in goodness, or perhaps to use your own goodwill to help another. Years dominated by the eleventh house may bring about really bright opportunities. As the house of wishes, things you once only dreamed of might actually be within reach. However, remember that "it depends" is the constant refrain of astrology. Truthfully, some of my most challenging years have been steered by the eleventh house, but that's because its ruler (a.k.a. co-creator) is in a tough spot.

The eleventh house is the place of alliances and people in high places who reach out a hand and help you advance. When you're in an eleventh-house year, goodness seems to flow to you through other people, whether they are friends, mentors, or community leaders. Speaking of friends, social and professional groups are also a main focus of the eleventh house. When this part of the chart is highlighted, friendship in its many forms can pop up. I've seen people meet lifelong friends or experience friendship breakdowns during eleventh-house times.

Good Spirit is also that unseen, unifying force that brings people together around a common cause, such as activism or advocacy. During an eleventh-house year, consider where you can use your gifts and privilege to lift up another.

• • • • • • • •

From My Case Files

When asked for her words of the year, Carina quickly said, "Gratitude, hopeful." She also mentioned a weakening of current friendships, offset by a strengthening of some childhood friendships.

Bunny spent the year exploring what delighted her, including painting, aerial yoga, and contemporary dance. She also had the opportunity to speak to several groups about her expertise.

From My Journals

In my first eleventh-house year, I had major friend drama. I was being bullied by a "frenemy" at school but also met a dear friend outside of school who made my life so much richer. In a later eleventh-house year, friend drama was a repeating theme, but besides that, a nonprofit I helped form received a historic mansion as a donation!

Reflection Questions

What do I want?

If what I want arrives, can I receive it?

Who believes in me? What can I learn from them?

Where can I find an ally, a mentor, or an advocate?

Where can I be an ally, a mentor, or an advocate?

How can I encourage or uplift someone else?

• • • • • • •

Twelfth House: Bad Spirit

Cadent, Unfavorable

Ages: 11, 23, 35, 47, 59, 71, 83, 95

Topics: Isolation and imprisonment, grief, anguish, loss, separation, endings, seclusion, childbirth, sorrow, suffering, illness, retreat, faraway places, enemies, self-sabotage

Twelfth-house years, like first-house years, are transitions. This is a time of bringing the last twelve years to an end. You're shutting things down and creating closure. It's not time to step forward but a time to turn inward and reflect on where you've been. This is an in-between space where something has ended but something new hasn't begun just yet. You may feel suspended between worlds, where you can intuit shadows of what's to come, but the vision isn't fully formed.

The twelfth house is one of the farthest, darkest corners of the birth chart, and during a twelfth-house year you can feel like you're far away or unreachable too. This may be a choice you make or something that forces you into "hiding." If you're naturally introverted, this time may feel like the medicine you need, but if you're used to being in the spotlight, it may feel like you're in the shadows no matter how hard you try to be seen. You may actually find yourself far away, traveling to a place very far from home, going on a retreat that's very foreign to your natural surroundings, or visiting a place of recuperation.

Twelfth-house years often correlate with a need to rest and recharge. The years surrounding it may have felt intense, pushing you to your limits, requiring you to pull back and take care of yourself or of another. I've noticed that twelfth-house years occasionally correspond with sacrifice and helping someone else through a time of sorrow. This can bring you to your own limits as well.

The twelfth house is a place of loss, grief, and suffering, and you'll typically find yourself journeying through the deep recesses of your mind and spirit. This is a year that brings spiritual and mental health into focus. You may be more interested in cultivating things that are unseen instead of working in the material realm, and your interest in metaphysical matters may increase.

Enemies also belong to the twelfth house, but they're often unseen. If you believe in ghosts and demons, this is where they reside. But these "enemies" could also take the form of secrets or other mental-emotional burdens. In modern times, the twelfth house has been aptly expanded to include the idea of inner demons or being your own worst enemy and how those fears or behaviors may isolate you.

From My Case Files

Charlotte dissolved her energy healing business and went back to her roots in public relations. When asked to sum up her year in one sentence, Charlotte said, "Deconstructing my inner system to realign, reigniting my creativity and purpose to make a difference."

Sarah chose the word *restriction* to sum up her twelfth-house experience. She expressed feeling isolated and limited not only by outside requirements on her time but by internal struggles like insecurity.

From My Journals

During my most recent twelfth-house year, I finished writing my first book and took a small sabbatical to recharge. I also made the difficult decision to finish my work in wellness and go in a new astrological direction, but I didn't quite know what that direction was yet.

Reflection Questions

Looking back over the last twelve years, what's been the connecting thread?

What am I bringing to a close?

How can I honor my endings and transitions? What do I need in order to feel complete here? What do I need for closure?

Where can I create more space for rejuvenation and recuperation?

What's exhausted? How can I care for this thing or part of myself?

• • • • • • •

Now that you've learned all about your house of the year, it's time to explore your planet of the year, or co-creator. Remember that your co-creator is the planet that defines how things feel and flow, so you want to know as much about its personality and desires as possible. In the following chapters, we take a deep dive into each co-creator, what to expect when it takes charge of the times, and how to work with it. You'll also find information on transits your co-creator might receive from other planets and how they could add to your story. Be sure to answer the reflection questions and do the planet channeling exercise at the end of your co-creator's chapter. It's one thing to have all the intellectual astrology pieces in place, but I encourage you to make space for your intuition as well, which is what these exercises are intended to do.

seven

Moon

Classification: Luminary

Topics: Inner terrain, emotions, body, mother, conception, travel, fluctuation and change, nourishment

You wake up in the middle of the night. Other than a sliver of moonlight, it's completely dark. You take some time to get your bearings and glance around before getting out of bed. The familiar room has turned into a collection of odd shapes and shadows. Walking slowly, careful not to bump into anything, you rely on your memory and outstretched hand to get to where you're going. Is that a chair? Is that the doorway or the wall? You're not entirely sure, but something tells you to take a step to the left.

This is what a Moon year can feel like. When the Moon's your co-creator, it can take some time to get your night-vision goggles on and adjust to the symbolic dark. Instead of clear, objective information, Moon years offer clues and maybes and nudges. But don't worry, you can still make it to your destination; you just have to lean on your felt sense and intuition.

The way you navigate life during a Moon-led year may be very different from your norm, especially if you have a day chart. Instead of making choices based on facts and figures, outside opinion, or what others are doing, you're asked to turn inward first. You may find that your decision-making process is very counter to what our solar culture recommends. When asked *why* you've made a certain choice, you may not have a "good" reason. You just know in your bones that you need to do this thing, and you need to do it in this particular way. And that's just fine. The Moon's way of operating is just as valid as the Sun's—it's just different. It steers with emotion and sensation instead of the mind.

Moon years provide opportunities to cultivate trust: trust in your inner knowing, trust in your body, trust in your own rhythms, and trust that just because you can't see something doesn't mean it's not there.

What to Expect During a Moon Year

The Moon symbolizes so many things in astrology, but I think it's most helpful to begin by remembering that it's the leader of the night club. Think about how your activities shift once the Sun goes down. What do you do at night? How do you spend your time? What do you think about and focus on? Unless you work the night shift, nighttime is typically more private and inward. Maybe you head home from work and put your stretchy pants on. You rest and refuel. You relax. You spend time with friends or family. You do your most intimate things and routines. This is the stuff of Moon years and what tends to take your attention when it's the Moon's turn to lead.

The Moon doesn't have its own light; it receives the light of the Sun. The Sun is an animating, outward-pushing force that values achievement and recognition—the things of daylight. The Moon, as its receptacle, represents the things that contain and support the Sun's light, like your body or your home. It's a physical, animal, tangible type of planet. Without the Moon, the Sun's ambition has nowhere to land and nothing to nourish it. During a Moon year, you may notice a need to take care of your life's supports more intentionally.

One of the Moon's major symbols is the physical body. During a Moon year, there may be a greater focus on your health and self-care routines. Sleep tends to top the list, as do food and emotional regulation. Caretaking in general may pop up when the Moon is in charge. This might look like an intense season of parenting, caring for aging parents, tending to a partner or friend in need, or, again, taking care of yourself in a deeper way.

Your home life and its relative comfort or discomfort may take center stage. The Moon wanders and moves, and your home life may also wander and move when it's activated. The Moon loves to nest, and when it's a co-creator, there's often a deep need to have a place to retreat. If you don't have this, you may be craving, perhaps even obsessed with, how you can find it. If you do have this, you might be spending a lot of time at home, whether that's wanted or imposed on you by outside circumstance.

This concept of home stretches to include the people you call home too. Whether it's chosen family or blood family, the Moon wants to belong. The Moon yearns for safety and security, and you may find yourself looking to others to fill this need. But ultimately, Moon years are about cultivating safety within yourself and getting the support you need to make that a possibility.

The Moon is about what's close and tender. It's your inner terrain, your secrets, your feelings that aren't always shared. Sometimes the Moon requests that you air this place out and bring it your full attention. This might mean navigating the lunar depths with a professional. How to be with difficult emotions and sensations is something the Moon loves to teach.

The Moon is a timekeeper, a planet of rhythm, and you may start questioning how you structure your time and if it feels supportive. You may notice that you want to find your flow and live in your unique rhythm—however that looks. Remember that being led by the Moon is very different from being led by the Sun's consistent schedule. The Moon has a repeatable, identifiable pattern, but it also changes daily. Give yourself permission to experiment with new ways of relating to time.

As a timekeeper, the Moon also holds your history. You may notice you're reflecting on your past, especially your childhood. Memories may be churning, and old feelings that weren't tended to at the time may come back around for resolution. The Moon specifically represents the mother, and it's natural for your relationship—or lack thereof—with your mother or a mother figure to become more central, whether in thought or reality.

The Moon represents anything that fluctuates, including mood, energy, interest, and motivation. It moves through the sky quickly, constantly changes, and connects with all the other planets at a rapid clip. You can feel like this too. Your moods and emotions may change on a dime; energy and motivation may fluctuate between extremes. You can't quite predict how you'll feel moment by moment. Moon years often require that you insert more buffer time into your schedule to make room for these frequent changes. It's also a call to trust in the Moon's promise: Waxing always follows waning, and fullness always follows emptiness. Feeling tired and depleted? The Moon gives you permission to rest without guilt or worry. You know that fullness will return. Feeling excited and energized? The Moon gives you permission to enjoy and embrace it. You know that it will eventually wane.

In the ancient world, the Moon was also a symbol of fortune and its mysterious tendency to fluctuate without warning. Depending on the condition of your natal Moon and your solar return Moon, you may notice an inflation or deflation of what you consider to be fortunate.

These are just a few of the possibilities that a Moon season may bring. But remember that the Moon also oversees personal themes in your birth chart. First, find the house that your natal Moon is in. Next, find the sign of Cancer, the Moon's domicile, in your birth chart and the house that it occupies. What life areas and topics does this house represent? These are the places that need nurturing and attention. These are the places that need rest and recovery. These are the places that need flexibility and care.

• • • • • • •

Reflection Questions

Explore the following questions and prompts at the beginning of your Moon co-creation cycle and reread them as time goes on. Notice if your answers change—this is totally expected, as the Moon changes rapidly, and you will too.

If I let myself be fully led by the Moon, what would change?

Where would I like to be more flexible with myself and allow for more fluctuation?

What in my life needs TLC, and how do I plan to deliver that?

How can I create more variety and flexibility in my schedule?

What did I need but perhaps didn't get as a child, and how can I give that to myself as an adult?

How would I like to bring more care and attention to my physical body this year?

Do I feel at home when I'm home? How can I make my space feel more like mine?

Moon Tips

- Revamp your bedroom and make it the most welcoming, calming space in the house.
- Prioritize your sleep health and get outside assistance if needed. Sometimes it can help to establish regular sleep and wake times, even on weekends.

- Start keeping a dream journal. Put a notebook by your bed and capture whatever images you can upon waking.
- Give yourself unconditional permission to change your mind as often as the Moon changes phases.
- Find a therapist who can help you unpack Moon themes like childhood and feeling safe in your body.
- Get a routine physical. (Remember, the Moon rules the physical body.)
- Organize your activities by the lunar cycle (see below).

• • • • • • •

Lunar Cycle 101

When the Moon is your co-creator, it becomes essential for you to watch its monthly cycle. New Moons, Full Moons, and especially eclipses tend to correlate with the main events of your year. Remember, you're plugged into the Moon in an intimate way right now, so its rhythm tends to become your rhythm. Getting to know the Moon's fluctuations will help you embrace and predict your own.

The most popular way to divide the lunar cycle is into waxing and waning halves, but my favorite way is to divide it into times of light and dark. There are times when the Moon is more light than dark and times when it's more dark than light. (Pro tip: The Moon can be dark but technically waxing, or bright but technically waning.) Just like you learned in the CLEAR method, when a planet is bright and visible, its expression is more public and outward, and when a planet is dark or invisible, its expression is more inward, and it does things in secret or at least more quietly. The same is true of the Moon.

You don't need some fancy astrology app to determine the Moon's brightness; a simple weather app will do. They usually list the visibility percentage of the Moon. If it's less than 50 percent, it's a dark phase. If it's more than 50 percent, it's a bright phase. Easy.

Dark Phases

New Moon, Waxing Crescent, Last Quarter, Balsamic (a.k.a. Waning Crescent)

Keywords: Invisibility, privacy, form, refinement, recovery

Remember the difference in priorities and activities when it's day versus night? You can use this same analogy to help you remember the difference between the Moon's light and dark phases. At night, you typically cultivate your most intimate relationships and attend to your private, inner life. You rest from this day and prepare for the next. Similarly, under the dark phases of the Moon, there's a theme of resting as preparation. You may notice a desire for more alone time, for more sleep, and maybe for taking a gentler approach to your to-do list. These are days for slowing down and replenishing. The dark phases carry a hush and give you an opportunity to eliminate excess noise and busyness, go inside, and reconnect with yourself.

These are also phases of processing. Think about dreaming—something you do every night so your brain can reorient itself and refresh. The dark phases of the Moon work in the same way. They help you sort, organize, and rejuvenate for when the Moon is big and bright again. Always remember that dark supports light. "Productivity" during the dark phases looks less like producing and more like refining, simplifying, and cleaning up what you've already done during the bright phases.

Light Phases

First Quarter, Waxing Gibbous, Full Moon, Disseminating (a.k.a. Waning Gibbous)

Keywords: Visibility, activity, ideas, creativity, energy

The bright lunar phases are associated with higher activity and visibility—doing things out in the world. When the Moon is full of light, life also tends to be full and busy. You may notice you have more energy and capacity. Want to put another thing on your to-do list? Go for it. Feel the courage to put yourself out there? Go for it. Want to share something that you've been holding close? Go for that too. These phases support you in bringing things into the light, and they're great times for sharing and getting feedback.

The bright Moon phases are also very generative, creative, and often ambitious times. Allow yourself to get swept up by their speed and vitality; it's totally okay to lean into that. You may notice that your mind is really active and full of ideas, and you may or may not have the focus to fully flesh them out. If not, just write them down and move on. Go where the juice and momentum are and let yourself explore and play.

When the Moon is your co-creator, try timing your life with the Moon cycle. In my first book, *Body Astrology*, I talked in depth about moving and nourishing your body in sync with the Moon, but that's just one possibility of many. For example, I'm writing this book using the Moon cycle as a guide. Play with syncing the following activities with the Moon cycle:

Movement: Try moving more frequently and perhaps more vigorously when the Moon is bright and with more gentleness and flexibility when the Moon is dark.

Creativity: Try rapid-fire creating when the Moon is bright—no inner critic, no holding back. Then, go back with a refining, editing eye when the Moon is dark.

Appointments and social engagements: Schedule the bulk of your social engagements when the Moon is bright and your personal care appointments when the Moon is dark. Play with generally scheduling less under the dark phases and perhaps scheduling more during the light phases.

Work tasks: Put more high-energy, high-visibility tasks on your to-do list when the Moon is bright and more recurring, detail-oriented, or inward-facing tasks on your to-do list when the Moon is dark.

What About Eclipses?

Eclipses are interruptions in the Moon's normal rhythm. They're like a blip on the radar or a skipped beat. If the Moon is your co-creator, eclipses may coincide with the major events or turning points of your year. Eclipses happen approximately every six months, and they come in pairs—a New Moon eclipse and a Full Moon eclipse. The entire four to six weeks surrounding the eclipses may feel supercharged. They can feel extra busy or as though things are tumultuous and topsy-turvy or both.

Eclipses are basically exaggerated New and Full Moons. Very simply, New Moons are about beginnings, and Full Moons are about culminations and therefore endings. Eclipses magnify these themes and make the beginnings and endings more obvious. Keep in mind that change *might* take place during the actual eclipse season, but it's just as possible for eclipses to act as whispers or seeds for change that will unfold over the next few months.

Eclipse season is an important time to up your self-care routine and strengthen your support system. Things can feel erratic and changeable, so give yourself as much stability and regularity as you can.

How to Keep a Moon Journal

The way your body and mind respond to certain Moon phases is unique and will be different from other people. The best way to personalize this information is to watch it in action. A Moon-ruled year is definitely the year to keep a Moon journal.

True story: Keeping a Moon journal was the thing that taught me the most about astrology. What I love about this practice is that it doesn't require any in-depth knowledge or fancy tools, but it still gives you really profound insight. You can be elaborate with your Moon journaling, and maybe that'll excite you during a Moon year, but you can also keep it simple. Try keeping a Moon journal for at least two cycles, ideally three, so you have data to compare.

In my very first Moon journal, I simply wrote the Moon phase at the top of the page and then did a free write. As my curiosity and astrological knowledge grew, I brought in the zodiac signs of the Moon. The Moon moves through a new zodiac sign about every 2.5 days. The zodiac sign of the Moon gives the day a certain flavor or tone. If the zodiac sign is like a song, the phase is how loud the song is playing. My free-writing practice was a fine place to start, but it made going back and analyzing the data a little challenging. So instead, after capturing some basic information about the Moon, I suggest you be a bit more fact-focused and objective. Then if you want to free write, go ahead and let it flow. Below is a basic template of what to capture in your Moon journal each day. Feel free to add your own questions if you want to track different things.

What's the Moon phase? Is this a bright phase or a dark phase? Is this a waxing phase or a waning phase?

What zodiac sign is the Moon in? What element is this sign associated with?

What's my energy level today? (Use a scale of 1 to 10 or choose words like *low*, *even*, or *high*.)

What's my dominant mood or emotion?

What did I do today? (A simple bulleted list is fantastic here.)

Free write from here if you wish.

At the end of a cycle, take some time to review your data and draw patterns. Here are some sample reflection questions:

Under which lunar phases (or signs) was I most energetic?

When was I more social or outward?

During which lunar phases (and/or signs) did I crave more rest?

When was I craving more alone time?

Transits to the Moon

While the Moon is your co-creator, transits from other planets (especially slow-moving planets) to your natal Moon are primary. They're the transits most likely to correspond with the main events or turning points of your year. These transits will affect the Moon's innate themes (body, nourishment, home, fluctuation, fortune) but also your Moon's personal themes based on what house Cancer occupies in your chart.

Moon-Moon

A Moon-Moon transit is called a lunar return, and it happens every month when the Moon returns to the same place it was when you were born. Lunar returns last just a couple of hours, but they may be a sensitive or sleepy few hours. These times are usually best spent relaxing and taking care of your body and spirit.

Mercury-Moon

Mercury gives a microphone to whatever planet it touches by conjunction or aspect. This transit lasts about a day and can really compel you to speak about what's deep within you, what's in your heart, and communicate what you need to yourself or others so that you can be taken care of.

Venus-Moon

When Venus connects with the Moon, themes of bonding and togetherness are reinforced. This is a great time for exploring what truly delights you, what brings you pleasure and makes you feel warm and fuzzy inside. It's also an interesting time to observe how you may sacrifice your own needs for the needs of others, whether in a balanced or unbalanced way.

Sun-Moon

A Sun-Moon transit just lasts a day and happens once a year. The Sun acts as a highlighter and brings whatever it touches into the spotlight. That means emotions, your inner world, your home life, and whatever else the Moon rules in your chart are up for review. The Moon prefers darkness, so when the Sun shines on it, you may feel a little bit exposed like your insides are on the outside. It's common to feel a bit more tender and emotional than usual.

Mars-Moon

Mars can really agitate and ruffle the Moon. During this collection of days, you can feel everything from energized and amped up to under attack and criticized. When Mars and the Moon are together, it's about feelings in motion. Sometimes getting into your body and using movement to process anything challenging can help. This is a good opportunity to befriend some of the more challenging feeling states, such as anger, resentment, stress, irritability, or rage. This face of your Moon is important to accept as well. Ask it what it needs and see what pops up.

Jupiter-Moon

Jupiter provides a nice Moon boost. During this transit, you may feel more buoyant or hopeful and as if life is full of possibilities. This is a great time to write some reminders for your future self, who is perhaps going through a rough patch, about how good life can be. This is also a nice time to explore taking a risk with your feelings, wearing your heart on your sleeve, and letting someone know how you feel.

Saturn-Moon

When Saturn touches the Moon, you may feel tender and like your emotions are unbearably heavy. Life can feel serious and burdensome, and you may be dealing with long-term commitments or situations that require a lot of focus or emotional labor. Circumstances may also feel limiting and restrictive. I remember when Saturn was on my Moon just a handful of years ago; I was not only in a work grind, but I also felt very isolated. When Saturn touches the Moon, it tends to make you feel separate and alone, even in a crowd. It's natural to want to hibernate during this time.

Uranus-Moon

The Uranus-Moon transit can be a fun one, but it can also be a little bit overstimulating. The Moon likes security and safety. Uranus likes anything but. When Uranus talks to the Moon, your emotions can feel erratic, your mind can change, and your routines can be turned inside out. This may feel welcome and therapeutic if the aspect is soft (trine, sextile) but may feel disruptive and destabilizing if the aspect is hard (conjunction, opposition, square).

Neptune-Moon

Neptune tends to exaggerate the Moon's emotional nature. These seasons can be overrun with compassion, sensation, or sensitivity.

Neptune has a flair for the dramatic. It's also a bit confusing and can make it hard for you to figure out which feelings are yours and which are someone else's. The line between self and other can get blurred, and you can end up taking care of everybody else but yourself.

Pluto-Moon

Pluto makes the Moon dig deep. These seasons, which may last a year or more, can feel a bit like a crucible or a proving ground. Pluto times are intense, but they can also squeeze out your inner gold and unearth your power and agency. I've experienced this transit as very maturing. Yes, it requires you to do hard things, but then you realize that you can do them, and you can do more. Pluto offers the Moon a threshold to walk through. It may enter the transit insecure and vulnerable and come out mighty and tenacious. These times can also cause you to become hyperfocused on one project or area of your life. I encourage you to go with the flow and let Pluto take you down to the depths—there's treasure at the bottom.

Moon Attunement and Channeling

You can do this activity with the intention of "meeting" your natal Moon, your solar return Moon, or both. I recommend doing both at different times and seeing what different messages and insights you get. For an audio version of this attunement, head to www.astrologywithclaire.com/cosmicyear.

• • • • • • •

Sit or lie down in a comfortable position. Take a deep breath, close your eyes, and settle into your body. Begin to notice the rising and falling that's already present in your body—the rising and falling of your breath, the rhythm of your heart.

Imagine being in the woods at night. Everything is hushed and peaceful. The birds have stopped singing; the creatures have gone to bed. It's just you and the moonlight. There's a path in front of you. You move forward using your hands as guides, noticing and delighting in the sounds of sticks and leaves crunching under your feet. There's no fear, just curiosity—what's at the end of the path?

Notice in the darkness that your other senses begin to pick up. Feel the air on your skin. Feel the path under your feet. Notice your vision adjust as you make out soft shapes and shadows. Notice your thinking mind begin to quiet as your intuitive body comes forward and leads the way.

You continue down the path, feeling calm and divinely guided. After you walk for a while, you come to a home in the woods. It can look however you like. Maybe it's a cabin with a thatched roof. Maybe it's a modern farmhouse with a red front door. It doesn't matter. Allow whatever's coming up to come up. This is where the Moon lives. It's where the Moon feels safe and cared for, and it has invited you in.

Open the door and take a look around. What type of decor is there? Maybe it's full of plush couches and floor pillows. Maybe there's a huge bed taking up most of the space. Maybe it's lit with candles. Decorate this space in whatever way pleases you and makes you feel comfortable and at ease, like you could take the best nap of your life.

After you've furnished the space, settle into the chair, couch, or bed that's most appealing to you. Notice that you're not alone. The Moon comes in through a door off to the side and smiles gently at you, welcoming you to the space. It heads to the kitchen to make you a cup of tea while you snuggle up in some blankets.

The Moon can take any form you like—person, animal, or otherworldly thing. Just allow your imagination to flow. The Moon asks you about your journey, what you felt and observed, and what's been going on in your life. There's a deep sense of caring emanating from the Moon; you know that you could say anything to it, and it would listen and accept you.

The kettle begins to whistle, and the Moon brings you a steaming cup of herbal tea. As the Moon hands you the mug, it deeply looks into your eyes. You feel the warmth of the mug in your hands and sink even deeper into a feeling of safety and relaxation. Then the Moon says, "I'm so glad you're here. I was hoping you'd visit me. I have some important things to tell you. I've been learning a lot about how you flow, your rhythm, and what you need to feel cared for, and I want to share that with you if that's okay. I also hear we're going to be spending some time together, and I'm thrilled. Here's what I've been dreaming up about our time together."

From here, grab your journal and write out what the Moon has to say. If you feel like the words aren't coming, or you get stuck, just describe what the Moon and its surroundings look and feel like. It's all valuable information.

Moon Prayers

Thank you, Moon, for showing me how to live in my unique flow.

Moon, I invite you to lead me back into flow. Thank you.

Thank you, Moon, for showing me that everything is made new again.

Moon, I invite you to bring peace and calm to this situation. Thank you.

Thank you, Moon, for showing me how to nurture myself.

Moon, I invite you to lead me to the foods and habits that are most nourishing for me. Thank you.

Thank you, Moon, for helping me embrace the phase that I'm in and for modeling that it's okay to show up with whatever level of brightness I have today.

Moon, I invite you to restore my body, mind, and spirit to fullness. Thank you.

eight

Sun

Classification: Luminary

Topics: Identity, core essence, vital force, reputation, honors, visibility, consistency, leadership, power, authority, mental perception, soul

Imagine walking into a room with floor-to-ceiling windows where the natural light is bright and ample. As the Sun streams through the glass, everything receives a warm glow. You grab a sunny spot on the couch, and when the light touches your face, your heart lifts with energy and possibility. You unclench your jaw, open your fists, and give your shoulders a roll. The warmth of the Sun melts away all tension and concern. Sitting here, you know deep within that everything is okay.

This is how it can feel to profect, or advance, into a Sun year. The cool, refreshing darkness of the Moon has given way to a clear morning. You feel rested and prepared to step back into the light of day—ready to shine and to share.

When the Sun is activated, themes of visibility, leadership, identity, personal image, vitality, and reputation tend to come to the forefront. Most of these themes come from the Sun's observable qualities. It's our most constant, vibrant light. It sits high in the sky, illuminates our world, and shines on everyone without bias. It's the organizing leader of our solar system and our source of life and warmth. During a Sun year, these solar qualities become alive in you too.

This increased visibility and brightness may feel welcome or awkward to you depending on the sect (a.k.a. club) of your chart. Just like a Moon year may feel better to those born at night, those born in the day tend to feel right at home when the Sun's in charge. They know the rules, and they're ready to step into the light and play. If you have a night chart, a Sun year still offers you major benefits, it just may take some getting used to. The Sun strives to be seen, to be known, to be celebrated, to advance and to lead, and that may be a stretch for a lunar personality. It can definitely be done; it just may not feel natural at first.

What to Expect During a Sun Year

According to Hellenistic astrologer Vettius Valens, the Sun is the light of the mind, it's mental perception. I like to think of it as the spark of life and consciousness that switches you on. It represents awareness, and that includes self-awareness and being able to see yourself clearly. When the Sun is activated, you may be asking big questions like *Who am I? Why am I here? How do I want to be known? What do I want to be known for? What lights me up? Where do I shine?*

The Sun upholds your image and reputation. It's how you are known among other people. Although it varies in intensity, Sun times may coincide with a period of redefining who you are and making major changes to the personal image you project. When the Sun is switched on, you may not only have the desire to reshape this image but in some cases may be called to defend it. (Sun years aren't always sunshine and rainbows.) Sometimes the Sun's brightness can bring unwanted attention or criticism too. Others may feel threatened by or jealous of your sudden self-assurance. But for the most part, people tend to report a feeling of truly "stepping into themselves."

Sometimes, Sun periods have a magical way of putting you in the right place at the right time. It's like the spotlight is finally on you (for better or for worse), and what you've been striving toward is finally getting its time in the Sun, its fifteen minutes of fame, its time of day—you get the idea. Sun years may show up as others finally recognizing how brilliant you are or as someone in a powerful position showing you favor. During Sun times, you're more magnetic and more likely to gain recognition and praise. The Sun's light naturally brings internal vision and clarity as well. This is a time of sharpening your focus, getting clear about where you're going, and moving forward with confidence.

Another core symbol of the Sun is leadership. It's the central force of our solar system, and all the other planets dance around it. Like the Sun, you too may find yourself in a position where other people or things are orbiting around you. You may be asked to take on a more prominent role at work or decide to step up and oversee something, or maybe you become a more central presence in your friend group.

The Sun and Moon are the vital lights, and they're the two planets that most readily represent your body. The Moon is the physical, earthen container that you're in, and the Sun is the spirit that fills it and brings it to life. When either the Sun or Moon is activated, vitality may emerge as a general theme, and occasionally a health matter may pop up. But when it comes to the Sun, spiritual and mental health tend to be emphasized. The Sun is your internal brightness, and depending on the astrological context, that brightness can be enhanced or dimmed during the Sun's year. Some Sun years are like fighting for your light, while others are like basking in your full glory.

And last but not least, don't forget that the Sun rules something very specific in your birth chart too. Check your chart for Leo, the sign ruled by the Sun. What house does it occupy, and what topics does this house represent? Managing those topics is your Sun's primary job, and when the Sun is your co-creator, these themes will come to the forefront. For example, if Leo is in your tenth house, not only will a Sun year bring about themes of visibility, identity, and reputation, but it'll also activate career (tenth house) themes.

• • • • • • • •

Reflection Questions

Explore the following questions and prompts at the beginning of your Sun co-creation cycle and reread them as time goes on.

Who are you?

What are you known for? Would you like to change this?

What lights you up?

What in your life are you ready to showcase? If the Universe shined a spotlight on you, where would you direct it?

What would you like to bring steady effort and consistency to during this time?

How do you feel about potentially being more visible this year? What's your comfort level with this? In what circles or contexts would you welcome this?

Where are you ready to take a leadership role?

Where do you shine? (Bragging encouraged.) How can you do more of this?

Sun Tips

- Put yourself first. Yes, really.
- Learn as much as you can about yourself and your personality. Do all the quizzes and get all the readings.

- Take a public speaking class, an acting class, or an equivalent that will make you get up in front of people and shine.
- Read memoirs and autobiographies and be inspired by other people's paths and choices.
- Take a trip to a sunny place.
- If it's safe for you, get a good dose of sunlight each day.
- Study the Sun. Watch it throughout the day, commune with it, and reflect on how the quality of sunlight changes throughout the year.
- Do an authenticity audit. If you're a business owner or a service provider, go back over your messaging and advertising materials and make sure they still feel like a pure reflection of who you are.
- Get your vision checked. (The Sun helps rule the eyes.)
- Actually celebrate your birthday this year. Throw a party and let people love on you!
- If it is safe for you, enjoy more cardiovascular activity. (The Sun rules the heart.)
- Surround yourself with bright colors. Maybe you buy a bright yellow journal this year instead of your usual black one (talking to myself), or you wear that red lipstick you've been hiding in the back of your drawer.

Living Seasonally

When the Sun is your co-creator, any movements the Sun makes will be more noticeable for you and may coincide with the major events or turning points of your year. By movements, I specifically mean the Sun's seasonal journey and its travel through the zodiac signs. Living seasonally isn't just a trendy idea during a Sun year, it's your reality. As the days grow in light, you too are growing in light, both inner and outer. And as the Sun sets earlier and rises later, you too may feel like you're waning in power.

You might also notice more sensitivity to the Sun's monthly sign switch. The Sun takes approximately thirty days to travel through one zodiac sign. As it does so, it also travels through your chart, going house by house, all the way around. The Sun acts as a highlighter or awareness-builder for whatever it's traveling through, and in reflection, you might benefit from bringing more attention to the house the Sun is currently in each month. Give it some TLC and spruce up the place. For example, as the Sun transits your first house, pay attention to your body and wellness routines, and as the Sun transits your second house, give more love to your finances.

Similar to a Moon year, eclipses (especially solar eclipses) will probably overlap with your busiest times and perhaps any changes or plot twists. When the Sun's light is interrupted or temporarily "turned off" in an eclipse, things can invert or feel a little choppy. Eclipses are just New and Full Moons times one thousand. New Moons correlate with beginnings, and Full Moons with culminations and eventual endings. During an eclipse, these beginnings and endings are magnified, become more noticeable, and sometimes unfold faster. Take some time to find out where the eclipses are occurring this year. What houses do they span in your natal chart, and what topics do these houses oversee? These are the life areas that will probably have the most activity, disruptions, or switch-ups.

Also mark your calendar for the months when the Sun will be particularly strong or weak. This depends on what zodiac sign it is in. Some zodiac signs bolster and enhance the Sun's natural qualities, while others inhibit them. I've listed these times below.

Sun in Leo

This is the strongest version of the Sun because it's the Sun's zodiacal home—it rules the sign of Leo. When at home, the Sun can be its true self. It's regal, royal, and clear but also playful and magnetic. It commands attention. As the real-time Sun transits through Leo, schedule your most outward-facing events or tasks. If you have something that requires a lot of visibility, star power, or courage, try doing it now or during Aries season.

Sun in Aries

This is the place of the Sun's exaltation. Just think about that word. It implies something high and lofty, placed above us all, maybe on a stage or a pedestal. When the Sun's in Aries, and it's your co-creator, you might enjoy increased attention and recognition—even if it's from yourself. It's possible you'll receive more respect or feel seen and heard on a level you haven't in the past. It's likely you'll also notice an improvement in the Leo-house topics of your chart during this time.

Sun in Libra

This is the place of the Sun's fall, which is opposite the place of its exaltation. Instead of being in a high place, the Sun is brought to a low place. This might manifest as a slight decrease in vitality and daily energy, a subtle dimming in future vision or enthusiasm, or, in some cases, a feeling of being overlooked or ignored. This can show up in how you treat yourself as well, as if you're giving your brightness away to everybody else, leaving nothing left over for you.

Sun in Aquarius

This is the place of the Sun's detriment, which is the opposite of Leo, the sign of its rulership. It means the Sun's as far away from home as it can get. In fact, it's in Saturn's home as a guest. Just imagine how awkward the Sun might feel in Saturn's home. Maybe Saturn lives in a dark underground space, with cold stone walls and floors, lit by dim candles. The Sun might feel squelched here—it can't reach its normal high and glorious place. Saturn has a lot of rules, too, and the Sun may feel limited by Saturn's bossiness. But one thing a planet in detriment is really good at is being creative and turning something difficult into something awesome. Enter this time with the problem-solving mindset of a mad scientist—you can figure this out. Eureka!

Transits to the Sun

While the Sun is your co-creator, transits from other planets (especially slow-moving planets) to your natal Sun are primary. They're the transits most likely to correspond with the main events or turning points of your year. These transits will affect the Sun's innate themes (identity, visibility, leadership, image, vitality) but also your Sun's personal themes based on what house Leo occupies in your chart.

Moon-Sun

This transit just lasts a handful of hours, but it may be a tender few. The Moon sensitizes whatever it touches and allows you to see the emotional needs of the planet it's interacting with—in this case, the Sun. The Sun wants to feel affirmed and accepted. This is a great time for self-care, journaling, or simply putting a hand on your heart and asking your Sun what it needs.

Mercury-Sun

The Mercury-Sun transit lasts about a day and is fantastic for self-expression. You may notice you're naturally more chatty and interested in connecting with others, specifically around sharing your story or thoughts. It's okay to talk about yourself! If you need to offer your opinion, give a presentation, write something important, or get something off your chest, today's a great day to do it.

Venus-Sun

This is a lovely spot on the calendar, and a great day for self-love. Make intentional time to enjoy the beautiful things in life. Go see some art, enjoy some live music, or treat yourself to whatever you find delightful. You may feel more magnetic and loved under this transit—relish the sweetness!

Sun-Sun

Happy solar return! Go through the birthday ritual in chapter 14 around this day.

Mars-Sun

The Mars-Sun transit typically lasts just a few days, but it can bring some major heat. The Sun is already hot, and Mars makes it that much hotter. This heat may simply show up as a very busy, supercharged handful of days. You may feel a surge of boldness or confidence. You might feel more assertive than usual and ready to put yourself out there. Occasionally, this could coincide with someone or something challenging your brightness.

Jupiter-Sun

Grab your sunglasses! The Jupiter-Sun transit is a beautiful one, and I hope you squeeze the most out of it. It can feel like a real boon. Enjoy increased vitality and a general feeling of hope and optimism. You may receive honors or recognition for something. You may be asked to take a more prominent role or receive a gift or even a promotion. There's a general feeling of encouragement and goodwill that comes along with this transit. Jupiter "puffs" the Sun up with hot air and lifts it high in the sky, where it (a.k.a. you) can be seen and celebrated. This elevation will last a couple of weeks. My first book was published during a Jupiter transit to my Sun, and it correlated with the natural outcome of a book launch (i.e., being seen more frequently by more people).

Saturn-Sun

The Saturn-Sun transit is one of the more challenging ones the Sun can receive. Sometimes it can feel like your inner or outer light is dimmed. This might literally show up as feeling invisible, like people just don't notice you and you're being overlooked, or as mental pressure and darkness. Saturn is very serious and can limit the Sun's rays and power. This may be a temporary time of testing or feeling blocked and constrained in some way. Where? Most likely in the Leo house area of life, but also in things like vitality, reputation, and visibility. During these times, you may be faced with an arduous task that requires a lot of hard work and endurance. You may feel like you're proving yourself. You might notice you're very hard on yourself during a Saturn-Sun transit—or somebody else is—and you expect a lot from yourself. It can push you to your limits both mentally and physically. Take heart; I believe that Saturn's ultimate goal is to build something that will last. And as parts of you feel like they're disintegrating or crumbling under Saturn's weight, trust that the pieces that are truly you, truly your essence, are being preserved and pressed into diamonds.

Uranus-Sun

Get ready for a "rebranding"! This can be an exciting time of self-discovery and change. You may start thinking of yourself in a whole new way and take on a whole new look to match. It's common for your interests to change too—go ahead and explore those wild ideas that you never expected to bring to fruition. Uranus values freedom above all else. This is a time of nonnegotiable autonomy and authenticity. What isn't right for you will be absolutely intolerable and may even make you sick to your stomach! Outdated identities and ways of being just won't cut it anymore. Now's the time to go out in a fresh direction, whether that's professionally, personally, or elsewhere (check your Leo house for ideas).

Neptune-Sun

Neptune casts a haze over the Sun, dispersing its light and making it hard to see. There's often a lack of clarity, and you might go off the path a tad (or in my case, a ton). I've made some really "interesting" decisions under a Neptune-Sun transit. "Interesting" here is a nice way of saying "not great." Neptune is full of mystery. You might be unsure of your direction, what you want, or where you're going. Neptune can also bring a season of lowered vitality, where your energy is elusive and comes and goes without warning. Occasionally, Neptune transits to the Sun may correlate with a disappointment, where the reality of something doesn't measure up to what you'd hoped. On the other hand, depending on the context, Neptune can also cast a glamour over the Sun, allowing you to charm and win people over with ease.

Pluto-Sun

This transit is a true reorganization of self. Your center can be totally rocked, or you may feel like you're existing without one for quite some time. Layers of identity peel off bit by bit. This is often a period of tearing down who you were so that you can build up who you are now. We tend to focus on the idea that Pluto destroys, but I want to remind you that it also resurrects. Pluto doesn't just take you on a trip to the underworld and leave you there. It also helps you reemerge into the land of the living. In some cases, Pluto can bring great magnetism and influence to your Sun. You may notice that your words and choices have magnanimous effects—that everything you do is dripping with power and is part of a grand, cosmic domino effect.

Sun Attunement and Channeling

You can do this activity with the intention of "meeting" your natal Sun, your solar return Sun, or both. I recommend doing both at different times and seeing what different messages and insight you get. For an audio version of this attunement, head to www.astrologywithclaire.com/cosmicyear.

• • • • • • •

Sit in a comfortable position. Take a deep breath and settle into your body. Take a moment to orient yourself to the space around you. Look in front of you, behind you, above you, and side to side. Turn your head fully to see that you are safe in this space. Feel your feet on the floor. Notice the points of contact between your feet and the floor below. Maybe wiggle your toes, adjust your feet if needed, and feel how the floor, and the greater earth below, holds you here.

Now bring your attention to your body. Notice that you're breathing and that you don't need to do anything to your breath. It is always here. Notice any places that feel tight and relax those areas further, making any small adjustments to feel more comfortable and at ease.

When you're ready, begin shaking out your hands like you're flicking off water, welcoming this movement in your body. Allow the movement to grow and expand and spread into your arms, into your shoulders, maybe even into your head and neck. Shaking and releasing, moving and unfreezing.

Notice any resistance to this movement, to this shaking, and just allow it to be present while you continue to make any spontaneous movements that your body wants to make. Allow any sounds, groans, or other noises that want to come out to do so. Slowly come to stillness when you feel complete.

Inhale and bring your arms out by your sides and over your head like a big sunrise. Then exhale, drop your arms, and let out an audible sigh. Do that again. Inhale, bringing your arms overhead like a big sunrise, then exhale, dropping your hands and letting out an audible sigh. And one more time at your own pace, bring your arms up, out, and over your head with a big inhale, then drop them as you exhale with an audible sigh, letting it all out.

Now imagine walking into a room with beautiful, floor-to-ceiling windows. The windows look out over your favorite place in nature. It's a bright, blue-sky day. The Sun is high in the sky and in its full glory.

There are two comfortable chairs in this room. Make them look however you like. Notice how the Sun is streaming through the window creating a warm, welcoming spot on one of the chairs. Imagine walking over to this patch of light and taking a seat. Feel the rays of the Sun on your skin. Allow the warmth to melt and relax any tension. Notice how your body feels here in this chair, in the sunlight, completely relaxed.

Now ask your inner Sun to come forward, to take a seat in the other chair in front of you. Trust whatever comes up. Maybe the Sun takes on a body. Maybe it looks like the actual Sun. Maybe it's a version of you. Or perhaps it's just a feeling. Again, trust whatever is coming up for you. What do you see?

Allow yourself to bask in this presence, to receive from the Sun. Notice how your body feels being with this central, constant, light, and warm presence. Notice the sensations in your body. Notice the quality of your breath and anything else that's coming up for you. This mature, calm, regulated, compassionate presence is your Sun. This is always within you. This is you.

Now imagine getting up out of your chair, walking over to the Sun, and merging with it, becoming one form, one entity—being fully engulfed by this shining presence. Now you're looking with the Sun's eyes. You see with the Sun's perspective. You have the Sun's wisdom and perception, its clarity and vision. You're now witnessing your life with the same light and warmth you were just basking in.

Pick up your pen and write down answers to these questions: What does the Sun have to say? What does the Sun see? What does the Sun know? Free write until you feel complete.

• • • • • • •

Sun Prayers

Sun, I step out of the way and let you lead. Thank you.

Thank you, Sun, for illuminating this for me.

Sun, I invite you to reorganize this for me. Thank you.

Thank you, Sun, for shining on me always.

Sun, I relax back into your light and warmth. Thank you.

Thank you, Sun, for your favor and elevation.

Sun, I invite you to bring clarity to this situation. Thank you.

Thank you, Sun, for brightening my mind and building my confidence.

nine

Mercury

Classification: Common (may act as a functional benefic or malefic)

Topics: Communication, knowledge, intellect, language, numbers, data, business and commerce, marketing, exchange, travel, motion

You're flying after that latte, in the best possible way. Your head is clear, you're fully awake, and you're ready to tackle your to-do list. In fact, you're looking forward to it. It's one of those days when you have lots of different things to juggle, but the variety feels exciting and interesting. You're bursting with ideas—thank goodness for sticky notes. Texts, calls, and emails are flooding in but instead of feeling like interruptions, they feel like inspiration. You're connected and you love it. You flutter from task to task with ease, not getting bogged down, following your flow, and feeling downright brilliant. This is a Mercury year at its best.

Mercury is a planet of change. Other than the Moon, Mercury changes its appearance the most frequently out of all the other planets. One day it's a morning star, one day it's an evening star. Sometimes it's bright and visible; other times you can't find it anywhere. One day it's moving forward, and another it's moving backward.

Mercury is a master of transformation and shapeshifting, and you may notice a desire or need to shapeshift along with it. Mercury tends to pivot rapidly from one thing to the next, and you may notice your life pivot in reflection from one focus to another. It's like juggling multiple plates in the air.

This busyness may be productive or not so much. I've had clients describe Mercury times as feeling like they're super busy but not accomplishing much or that there's a lot going on but it's not what's most important. In my most recent Mercury year, I was juggling a lot of commitments, and although I was able to finish the one thing I deemed most important, it took me a really long time to complete because I was so distracted by other things.

Focused, active, fast, clear. These are some of the words that come to mind when I think about Mercury. But their opposites can also show up: distracted, sluggish, slow, foggy. Which ones will dominate? Well, it depends. How a Mercury year feels hinges on the greater astrological context, a.k.a. Mercury's condition in your natal chart and in your current year's solar return. (Head back to chapter 3 for more info on this.)

What to Expect During a Mercury Year

Mercury is the planet of communication, language, writing, thinking, motion, and travel. Beyond the topics of your house of the year, these are the themes most likely to fill your days.

Communication has the green light this year. This could show up in a simple, straightforward way, like receiving more emails or attending more meetings than usual, but there's usually a deeper layer. The way you talk to others and the way you talk to yourself tends to be up for review. There's often an internal audit of your thoughts and conditioning. You may spend a lot of your Mercury year thinking about thinking. Why do you think the way that you do? Where did you pick those patterns up? And do you still want to believe them or carry them forward?

Mercury years can also be pretty noisy. You may be on the receiving end of a lot of opinions or questions, and although this can feel really interesting and stimulating, it might also feel distracting or annoying. Taking regular, intentional time away from your phone and from television, podcasts, and social media is basic self-care when Mercury rules the calendar and can keep you from getting lost. Mercury is a chameleon, and it can be easy to take on other people's thoughts as your own. A question I often use during Mercury times is, *Is this information for me or for someone else?*

When Mercury is co-creator, there's usually a huge craving for new knowledge. It's common to take a bunch of classes, start a formal program of study, or even begin learning a new language. Mercury wants to know everything, and it wants to know it now. It's the planet with a stack of seven books on its nightstand, all in various stages of completion. Mercury is the quintessential multitasker.

But Mercury doesn't just like to receive information; it likes to share it too. I've seen several clients dive seriously into writing during Mercury years, whether it's a book project, a blog, or a journaling practice. Mercury is a storyteller, and when your Mercury is switched on, it's common to feel like sharing yours, whether it's through the written word, a podcast, or social media. Mercury loves to chitchat and share via technology.

Mercury is a planet of exchange, and yes, this means information, but it also means goods and services. This planet means business, and when it's activated, you may notice increased themes around buying and selling. It's also a time for gathering data, sorting through that data, and noting patterns so that you can make informed decisions. Organization projects are ripe and ready to be tackled this year. If you're an entrepreneur or service provider, this year might be about crunching the numbers, adjusting your systems and workflows, or tweaking how you connect with your current and potential customers through language.

Don't forget that Mercury rules something very specific in your birth chart too. Check your chart for the signs of Gemini and Virgo. What houses do they occupy, and what topics do these houses represent? Managing those topics is your Mercury's primary job, and when Mercury is your co-creator, these themes will come to the forefront.

• • • • • • •

Reflection Questions

Explore the following questions and prompts at the beginning of your Mercury co-creation cycle and reread them as time goes on. Expect your answers to change as Mercury does!

What would I like to organize this year?

What would I like to learn more about this year?

What's the status of my mental health, and how can I support it more directly this year?

What information do I consume? Does this feel good, and do I want to continue consuming it?

How do I speak about myself to myself and to others? Would I like to make any changes here?

As the year gets busy and full, what's the number one reminder I want to carry with me?

What stories or information do I want to share, and how do I plan on sharing it?

What's my Mercury retrograde plan for the year? What am I going to use it for? (Keep reading for more information on Mercury retrograde.)

Mercury Tips

- After answering the question above about your number-one reminder, write it on a notecard or make some digital art and put it as the background on your phone and computer so you can see it as often as possible.
- Mercury loves to read. Get a library card and pick up a stack of books. Ask Mercury to guide you through the shelves to whatever's fresh and inspiring.
- If you're writing and feel stuck, take Mercury on a walk. Open the voice recorder on your phone or use the talk-to-text feature to capture your ideas.
- Mercury thrives on variety and activity. Make regular dates to get out of your house or office and visit your favorite café.
- Take regular, mini "information fasts" during which you refrain from consuming content so that you can reimmerse yourself in your own thoughts and ideas.
- Do a social media audit and unfollow any accounts that no longer inspire or encourage you.
- Put boundaries around your phone use and try to keep it in a separate room while working and sleeping.
- When making a to-do list, give yourself a "menu" of options and allow yourself to flutter between tasks.

What About Mercury Retrograde?

When Mercury's your co-creator, you guessed it: Mercury retrograde matters more than usual. Mercury retrograde is when it looks like

Mercury changes direction and moves backward. It's classically associated with delays, communication snafus, and frustration. But don't worry! It can be an exceptionally productive time if you know what to do with it. Mercury retrograde happens a lot—approximately four times per year for about three weeks a pop. That's a lot of retrograde time each year, so it's a good idea to make friends with it. The sections below provide six Mercury retrograde strategies for you to play with.

Be Open to the Retrograde Muse

When Mercury switches directions, you may switch directions too. What you're working on or interested in may lose its luster and a new something could drop in. This is okay! Don't force yourself to stick to business as usual during the retrograde. Be open to the retrograde "muse." Give yourself these weeks to follow any new threads that Mercury presents. You won't get lost because you've written your reminder of what's most important this year, remember? Mercury retrograde is simply a time to check in and ask, *Does this direction still resonate and feel true to me, or do I want to go with the new thing that Mercury's offering right now?*

Do It Differently

You don't have to completely stop what you're doing during a retrograde, but you may need to come at it from a different angle, especially if you find yourself getting stuck—not uncommon during these times. Doing it differently might mean doing your normal thing backward, coming at something from the side, or trying something you've never done before.

Go with the Slow

You have permission to stop fighting against a retrograde and just slow down. Sometimes I like to think of a planet's retrograde cycle as each planet's opportunity to go on vacation and recharge. When you think about it that way, it doesn't sound so bad, right? Sure, you can try to hustle during a retrograde—knock yourself out. But you may actually knock yourself out, meaning you may feel like you're hitting tons of walls and unnecessary setbacks. If you just chill out, and go with the slow, remembering that it's only temporary, you have the potential to remove all that unnecessary suffering in an instant.

Beta Test

I've used retrogrades many times to beta test a class, service, or other project. It's a low-pressure way to gather information about something you're interested in doing without too much risk in the form of energy or time. Again, retrograde does not mean you have to sit on your hands and do nothing. These are wonderful chunks of time for experimentation.

Reduce, Reuse, Recycle

By *reduce*, I literally mean reducing your workload if possible. In my experience, we tend to have more limited bandwidth during retrogrades, or our bandwidth fills up faster. I like to be kind to myself and preserve my bandwidth by consuming less outside information and removing tasks that are just extra pressure. Reduce could also refer to cleaning something up or refining and simplifying something, like editing a document, cleaning up the files on your computer, or putting the finishing touches on a proposal.

During a retrograde, Mercury is retracing its steps through the zodiac. It's like a second chance. What a wonderful opportunity for you to try or use something again. Retrogrades are my favorite times for reviewing all of the wonderful things I've already made and considering if there's anything I'd like to dust off and refresh. Whether it's old social media posts or searching for last year's recipe stash, retrogrades encourage you to use what you've already got.

Wait It Out

Taking a conscious pause on something until Mercury retrograde passes is perfectly reasonable and okay. I've done this often, sometimes as a choice and sometimes not; but even if I didn't choose the pause, it worked out for the better. To be clear, I'm not pausing out of fear but out of wisdom. I've learned from observing many Mercury retrogrades that occasionally I simply don't have all the information I need during a retrograde to move forward with clarity and ease.

Mark Your Calendar: Mercury Cazimi

Beyond Mercury retrograde, another thing to mark on your calendar is a bright spot called Mercury cazimi. This is when Mercury is exactly conjunct the Sun. Astrologers call this being "in the heart of" the Sun. Think of the Sun as a monarch or a representation of divinity. When Mercury is cazimi, it's like this divine figure fully welcomes Mercury into its inner sanctum. The Sun shares its secrets, its wisdom, and its wealth and allows all Mercury things to flourish.

When Mercury is your co-creator, you might notice a nice boost on these days. Mercury cazimi is a fantastic time for getting clarity and making a decision. It's also perfect timing for any and all Mercury things, ranging from writing and speaking to business dealings and social events. When Mercury cazimi happens during Mercury retrograde, it's like a get-out-of-retrograde-free card. This is the one day during the retrograde when things may start to make sense if they've been foggy.

Transits to Mercury

While Mercury is your co-creator, transits from other planets (especially slow-moving planets) to your natal Mercury are primary. They're the transits most likely to correspond with the main events or turning points of your year. These transits will affect Mercury's innate themes but also your Mercury's personal themes based on what houses Gemini and Virgo occupy in your chart.

Moon-Mercury

If the Moon represents your emotional body and Mercury represents your mental body, then a Moon-Mercury transit brings the two together. During this handful of hours, you may feel more in tune with your emotions, perhaps feeling the need to process them through journaling or with a friend or loved one. The Moon can make Mercury a tad subjective, so this isn't the best time for very clear thinking or decision-making, but it's perfect for going inside and seeing what you need to feel supported.

Mercury-Mercury

Mercury-Mercury is a very active transit in which your mind moves a mile a minute. This time is great for getting things sorted and organized. Channel this buzzy energy into creating a system that Mercury would be proud of, whether it's reorganizing your pots and pans, color-coding your books, or writing an outline for your next short story. This is also a terrific transit for communication and business transactions of all kinds. When Mercury lights up your natal Mercury, you may also notice clues or new insights about your unique communication style and how you express yourself best.

Venus-Mercury

This is a lovely transit in which Venus brings good cheer and beauty to the mind of Mercury. You might feel like you're wearing rose-colored glasses on this day and may also notice it's easy to be more loving toward yourself and those around you. It's a fantastic time to create something beautiful—write some poetry, compose a song, do some painting. One very literal translation of this transit is "beautiful words." This is a time for sharing words of love and care with others through whatever medium delights you.

Sun-Mercury

I like to think of the Sun-Mercury transit as sunshine brightening and uplifting the mind. It can be a real mood booster. When the Sun, which represents your divine essence and identity, comes to Mercury, there's an opportunity to put more of yourself into everything you do. This is a classic transit of self-expression and being authentic with your words. This transit also carries a similar imprint to Mercury cazimi, where the Sun offers Mercury (a.k.a. you and your mind) insights that it may have missed. The Sun brings light to all the corners of Mercury's sphere, allowing you to see clearly and have plenty of aha moments.

Mars-Mercury

This short transit can feel very high energy and sometimes overstimulating or irritating. Make sure you have an outlet, both physical and mental, so that you can soar through this time with inspiration and vitality. I love this transit and find that it fills me with a get-up-and-go feeling. I'm rarely at home when Mars visits my Mercury; I'd rather be exploring. Mars can help Mercury cut through the noise and get to the essentials. If you need to say something bold, cut ties, clarify, or simplify, now's a great time to do it.

Jupiter-Mercury

When Jupiter visits Mercury, Mercury's already hefty thirst for knowledge and information becomes insatiable. This transit often overlaps with an enthusiastic time of learning or teaching. You might be in a season of thinking outside the box or exploring new-to-you ideas and philosophies that are blowing your mind. This transit also reminds me of a megaphone. Jupiter takes Mercury's message and broadcasts it for everyone to enjoy. Have something to share? It'll probably be widely and well received under this transit.

Saturn-Mercury

Saturn tends to slow Mercury down and make it more serious. This transit may coincide with a head-down period of focus or study. There may be an important body of work that you're putting the finishing touches on, or you may be sorting through papers or finalizing the details of something significant. This is a good time for anything that requires a lot of attention to detail and a critical eye. But this critical eye can turn inward as well and show up as a time of self-censorship or insecurity, and instead of a flood of ideas (something that Jupiter-Mercury might bring), you may feel that they're few and far between.

On a subtler level, this may be a time when you feel more reserved, and occasionally this transit can come with a bit of sadness. The areas of your chart that Mercury oversees may feel squeezed or blocked. You may feel like no matter how hard you try, nothing seems to budge, or it requires a lot of effort to move an inch. But this can also be a very productive and maturing time if you're willing to show up for the hard work. I remember during a recent Saturn-Mercury transit, I got very serious about relating to myself as a writer, and I decided that writer's block didn't exist for me anymore. I learned how to sit down and write on command, whether or not I felt like it. Very Saturn.

Uranus-Mercury

Get your notebook ready! This transit can feel like you're a mad scientist on the brink of a eureka moment. All the ideas tend to come flooding in at once. This time period is definitely not boring and will keep you on your toes. Things are busy, frenetic, and a touch wild. Be sure to take some time to unplug or else you may get zapped. You may notice an itch to change your mind about something pivotal during this time. This is usually because when Uranus is in town, authenticity becomes nonnegotiable. It may feel urgent that you be your full self and express that self freely, no matter what the fallout may be.

Neptune-Mercury

This can feel like a very long Mercury retrograde. Instead of clear thinking and quick movement, this time period may feel foggy and confusing, like you're driving in circles. Instead of pressuring yourself to get clear, ask for help. When I'm having a Neptune transit, I like to get trusted outside opinions on any life decision; otherwise, I may end up somewhere unintended.

Words not coming to you? That's normal! Express yourself through art, music, movement, or film. If you do want to write or journal, allow yourself to just let it out via stream of consciousness and don't force it to make sense. It's also wise not to believe everything you think or hear during this time. Take time to validate the information that comes your way and make sure it's relevant for you.

Pluto-Mercury

This transit is all about truth and depth. There's no room for small talk here. When Pluto touches Mercury, you may notice your mental world is captivated by something very specific. This is a transit about specialization, not generalization, and it often comes with obsessive deep dives and rabbit holes. There's an intense need to know and understand. You may feel compelled to get to the bottom of something or figure out the truth.

There's also a tendency to become very private and perhaps secretive or protective of yourself during this time. You may feel the need to isolate and may hesitate to share your thoughts unless they're absolutely "perfect" or "pure." I like to think of Pluto as the makeover planet, and when it comes to spruce up Mercury, it may coincide with a deep "makeover" or examination of your mental health and thought patterns with a professional.

Mercury Attunement and Channeling

You can do this activity with the intention of "meeting" your natal Mercury, your solar return Mercury, or both. I recommend doing both at different times and seeing what different messages and insights you get. For an audio version of this attunement, head to www.astrologywithclaire.com/cosmicyear.

• • • • • • •

Sit or lie down in a comfortable position. Take a deep breath, close your eyes, and settle into your body. Imagine walking into a home doubling as a tech startup. You hear binaural beats, coffee brewing, keystrokes, and notification pings. People are all over the place, devices in tow, super focused on what's in front of them. The energy here is exciting and makes the hair on your arms stand on end.

You spot Mercury at a corner desk in the back. It's surrounded by all kinds of gadgets, plus a stack of papers and books. Mercury is on the phone but sees you coming and motions you over. As Mercury talks on its earbuds, it's also typing and jotting something on a sticky note, as if it has three hands. You pull up a chair next to Mercury and notice that it's got at least ten tabs open, plus a few documents in various stages of completion.

"They just walked in," Mercury says, speaking about you. "Yes, I'll be sure to tell them everything. Okay, bye."

Finally, Mercury turns to you with undivided attention and says, "I just got off a conference call with all the other planets, and have I got news for you. Let's head to the boardroom, and I'll tell you everything I know."

You take a notebook and pen out of your bag and walk into the kitchen, which doubles as the boardroom. You take a seat at the table, and Mercury serves you both a steaming cup of coffee, black.

"So," Mercury says, "we were chatting about your upcoming year and how I'm going to be helping you steer things as your co-creator. But you know me, I couldn't help calling up everyone else and hearing their thoughts on what to focus on this year. It's been hard to whittle things down because I'm so excited to be your co-creator, and I want to do a lot of things together. But here's what I've got so far."

Mercury pulls up the minutes from the planetary conference call on its tablet and turns it toward you. There are five things on the list. What are they? Free write until you feel complete. Be sure to thank Mercury for sharing its insights with you.

• • • • • • •

Mercury Prayers

Thank you, Mercury, for guiding me to the information that's most relevant for me right now.

Mercury, I invite you to help me view this situation with clarity. Thank you.

Thank you, Mercury, for helping me see this situation objectively.

Mercury, I invite you to fill my mind with bright ideas. Thank you.

Thank you, Mercury, for connecting me with the right people and opportunities.

Mercury, I invite you to reorganize this for me. Thank you.

Thank you, Mercury, for allowing my words to be well-received.

Mercury, I invite you to bring brightness and flexibility to my mind right now. Thank you.

ten

Venus

Classification: Benefic

Topics: Relationships, love, desire, romance, friendship, beauty, pleasure, fun and leisure, art and music, appearance, style, magnetism, passion, money

As I sit down to write this chapter, I've got some French pop playing, a fresh matcha latte at my side, and a feeling of gratitude that I get to wake up this morning and do my favorite thing. I'm at a vacation rental in the mountains for the weekend, and the change of scenery is just what the muse ordered. The sun is out, the birds are singing, I have my favorite comfy sweater on—all the details are just right. Like this moment, a Venus year is an opportunity to connect with the little luxuries and pleasures of life. Venus years happen either after the busyness of a Mercury year or the heat of a Mars year, and it's like coming to an oasis in the desert. This is a time of slowing down and repairing. Of course, there are always exceptions, but generally, this is a very good place to start.

One of my favorite ways to learn about the planets is to watch period piece dramas and imagine which planet would play which role. Remember that Venus is a member of the night "club," meaning it answers to its club captain, the Moon. The Moon is queen, and I like to think of Venus as Queen Moon's most trusted attendant or lady-in-waiting. Venus does Queen Moon's hair, picks out her gowns, accompanies her on promenades, and comforts her with song and dance during times of sorrow. As Queen Moon's trusted friend, Venus benefits from the queen's high rank and also has access to gorgeous gowns, the richest food, and the most luxurious accommodations. When we use this analogy, we see Venus's topics from relationships and appearance to pleasure and art pop out right away.

What to Expect During a Venus Year

Venus's most popular association is with romantic love, but it rules all types of connections, including friends, acquaintances, and business partners—it's a planet of alliances. Venus years tend to bring one or several of these connections into the spotlight. Ideally, Venus years are a time for deepening and nourishing these relationships, but Venus years aren't always a cakewalk. How relationships will feel and fare depends on Venus's "happiness" in your natal chart and in your solar return chart, as well as your transits. For example, I suffered my first teenage heartbreak during a Venus year, a broken engagement in another, but in a later Venus year I got engaged to my now husband. As you can see, Venus highlights relationships, but the outcome can be a mixed bag.

Venus rules pleasure, and you might feel the nudge to indulge a bit more in the goodies life has to offer during Venus's reign, and I encourage you to follow that. Venus gives you an opportunity to explore not only what feels good but what you desire. Depending on your natal chart, this exploration may be natural or a little awkward. What's interesting about Venus's strategy for getting what it wants is that it's rather passive. It receives. Venus is exceptionally magnetic. It doesn't go out and make things happen—that's something a planet like Mars would do. Rather, Venus lies back on its chaise lounge and allows people and opportunities to come to it. Similarly, I encourage you to find a way to relax back and allow life to flow to you instead of pushing forcefully forward.

Instead of hustling, you can usually find Venus playing games or doing crafts. Venus is a master artist and delights in filling your hands with skill and your eyes with beauty. A Venus year is a great time to reconnect with an old hobby or to find a new one. I remember one Venus year ages ago, I was dreaming about being a professional musician and dabbling in all kinds of outdoor sports until I found the one that felt just right. I was also spending a lot of money keeping those hobbies up—another thing Venus loves to do.

Venus is also a symbol of beauty and adorning the body. A Venus year is a fantastic time to up your self-care game a bit. Refresh your wardrobe, explore vibrant colors, and try that new hairstyle you've been thinking about. Side note: Depending on Venus's placement in a chart, it can get very mixed up in societal definitions and expectations of beauty and gender roles. My point is: Venus rules over customs, decorum, and etiquette—how things are done in a culture and what's expected of you to keep up appearances. During a Venus year, you get to decide if you want to play this societal game or not.

Venus is a little bit like Goldilocks. It likes things to be "just right." It's obsessed with harmony and loves the idea of "balance," no matter how much of a myth balance may be. When Venus rules your time, it's easier to see what feels out of whack, whether it's too much or too little. Aim for a state of homeostasis and play with tweaking all the little details until life feels like it flows.

And finally, don't forget that Venus rules something very specific in your birth chart too. Check your chart for the signs of Taurus and Libra. What houses do they occupy, and what topics do these houses represent? Managing those topics is your Venus's primary job, and when Venus is your co-creator, these themes will come to the forefront.

• • • • • • •

Reflection Questions

Explore the following questions and prompts at the beginning of your Venus co-creation cycle and reread them as time goes on.

What brings me joy right now, and how can I fit more of this into my life?

Where would I like more human connection, and how can I begin to cultivate this?

What would I like to create this year? What is my "art"?

What relational boundaries do I need to set in order to feel at peace this year?

What hobbies have I been curious about? What's the first step in making one of these happen?

What's my definition of pleasure? How can I weave this into my day-to-day?

What feels out of balance in my life, and what would it look like if it were in harmony? (Be specific.)

I want . . .

Venus Tips

- Venus is all about the little luxuries. Upgrade your routines with small touches like a coffee mug that makes you feel like you're at a Parisian sidewalk café.
- Add a splash of Venus to your workday by swapping your black ballpoint for a variety of colorful gel pens.

- Try out some new hobbies. Curious about that ballet class? Painting? Pottery? This is the year to dabble in something artsy and fresh.
- Plan a getaway with friends and nurture the relationships in your life.
- Venus loves to look its best. Prioritize personal grooming appointments. Yes, actually get that regular hair trim and pedicure.
- Do a Venusian closet clean-out. Invite Venus to help you sort through your clothes and donate the ones that no longer excite and delight you. When you're ready to refresh your wardrobe, take Venus shopping, asking it to guide you to the clothes that'll make you feel the most at home and confident in your body.
- You're naturally more magnetic this year and primed to make connections, but you have to leave the house. Take yourself on dates, putting yourself in places where you're more likely to meet new people.

• • • • • • •

What About Venus Retrograde?

Venus stations retrograde about every nineteen months for approximately six weeks apiece. Venus might not have a retrograde cycle while it's your co-creator, but if it does, definitely mark your calendar. Some basic retrograde keywords that you can layer on top of any of Venus's symbols include *delay, detour, alternative, slow, wait, pause, refine, redesign,* and *restore.* Basically, when retrograde, the things Venus rules (connection, pleasure, creativity, beauty, desire) slow down or experience some other type of change. The things that Venus usually feels confident handling suddenly feel a little different. Venus doesn't really know how it wants to act or dress or create in this new environment, but it can figure it out, right?

During Venus retrograde, Venus topics may waver or feel inconsistent, like an on-again-off-again relationship. There may be an instability or a messiness to things that are typically smooth, and it can be easier to see what feels off instead of what's working. Venus topics like relationships or creative projects may require a new approach. You might notice where connections have broken down and need repair. Or you might notice where there's a mismatch of values—for example, a discrepancy between what you say you want and what you're actually doing.

Here are a few of my favorite Venus retrograde reflection questions: *Is this still important to me? Do I still want this? Does this still feel good?*

Transits to Venus

While Venus is your co-creator, transits from other planets (especially slow-moving planets) to your natal Venus are primary. They're the transits most likely to correspond with the main events or turning points of your year. These transits will affect Venus's innate themes (relationship, art, praise, pleasure, culture, etc.) but also your Venus's personal themes based on what houses Taurus and Libra occupy in your chart.

Moon-Venus

This is a short transit, lasting just a few hours. You might notice you feel the desire to connect deeply with the people or animals in your life. This transit is about togetherness and replenishment. Instead of being really active and go get 'em, this time might feel more natural for unwinding and recovering from the hubbub of life.

Mercury-Venus

When the planet of communication activates Venus, it's time to share good news and create beautiful things. Mercury hands a microphone to Venus and asks it to spread its message of love. This is a good time to tell others how much you appreciate them. It's also an opportunity to get clear on what you value and to make sure your message (Mercury) aligns with your heart (Venus). Mercury also tends to take Venus on the go. This is a great day to explore a new place in nature or simply head to that new café on the corner—you never know who you'll meet or what'll delight you.

Venus-Venus

This is a really beautiful transit that brings in all the best Venus has to offer. This is a great time to be social, host a party, or just surround yourself with the finer things in life. Whatever Venus represents in your life (check the houses that Taurus and Libra occupy) may experience a positive boost. It's also a wonderful time to love on your body and appearance, whether that's buying a new outfit or getting your hair done. I remember during one of my recent Venus-Venus transits, I got obsessed with finding the perfect foundation. I got lost in a YouTube rabbit hole watching makeup tutorials and spent the day shopping. That may sound a little silly, but most of the time, short transits simply show up as passing moods and activities.

Sun-Venus

This transit is a lovely blip on the cosmic radar. Confidence is high and magnetism is higher. Sun-Venus combinations create a lot of attraction. You might notice people are really interested in you today or that you get some type of recognition or appreciation. This can also be a fantastic moment for creative self-expression. Pull out your art supplies or grab your guitar and let yourself shine.

Mars-Venus

Mars can bring an unstable and erratic feel to Venus. Venus's topics may feel hot and cold—one day you're really into something and the next you couldn't be bothered. Mars excites Venus and makes it a little impatient. You may notice you want to jump into connections, collaborations, or projects without really thinking them through. If you can, take a moment to pause and make sure what you're saying yes to really aligns with your values and that you have an exit strategy in case things don't go as planned.

Mars can also bring some heat to relationships. Depending on the context, this can feel like an electric charge between you and another person or like friction in the form of a rivalry or disagreement. There could even be some jealousy in the mix. Basically, Venus things are hot right now and that means that sometimes they can burn. This transit may highlight a challenge in a connection that needs to be smoothed over and addressed. It may show differences of opinion, approach, or value—sometimes opposites attract, but sometimes they just repel.

Jupiter-Venus

This is one of the juiciest astrological combinations you can have. Squeeze the most out of it! When both benefic planets are in aspect, the most pleasurable and beautiful things in life are usually within reach. When Jupiter comes to Venus, there's a great opening up and broadening of horizons. Jupiter elevates Venus and increases its magnetism and power to attract. You may feel like people are drawn to you or as though opportunities are falling into your lap. Life can feel like a series of green lights. Jupiter also tends to stretch and grow Venus—this usually feels subjectively positive, but sometimes there can be a few growing pains. Jupiter multiplies the topics of Venus, and this may look like an increase in the number of people in your life or an upgrade in the caliber of connections.

Saturn-Venus

This is one of the more challenging transits to Venus. Saturn is a planet of isolation and separation, while Venus is a planet of togetherness and connection. As you can see, these planets are relational opposites and want different things, which can make it difficult for them to compromise. When Saturn touches Venus, feeling lonely, even among a group of people, is possible. You might be literally or figuratively cut off from your loved ones, desire more alone time, or feel like your needs aren't being met in a relationship. Sometimes this transit may correlate with feeling unsupported in your current connections and is an opportunity to learn how to fully support and value yourself no matter what the people around you are doing. This transit often kicks up the hard work of relating—it's a reality check or reminder that sometimes good things require effort. This is a rich time for creating and asserting relational boundaries. It's also a good time for restructuring a relationship and making sure that expectations and roles feel fair. It's a season of maturing and refining your connections. Sometimes when Saturn comes to Venus certain alliances and connections fall apart. The way I make peace with this is to choose to believe that the connections or projects that aren't in my long-term interest and aren't strong enough to support me will disintegrate, and those that will continue to lift me up for many years to come will survive.

When Saturn touches Venus, sometimes what you want is pushed aside for what is necessary. Pleasure often feels replaced by duty, responsibility, and obligation. This is a transit of commitment and going the distance with a person or project. You may have to say no to the many ideas to focus on the one essential connection or priority.

Uranus-Venus

Depending on the context, this can be a really fun and exciting transit. When Venus and Uranus come together, it's like throwing a surprise party. Uranus brings twists, turns, and rollercoaster-ride experiences. When it touches Venus, Venus topics like relationships, values, desires, and fun need to buckle up and keep all arms and legs inside the vehicle. New connections may seem to come out of nowhere. They can be thrilling, but they may also feel a little unstable, like you never really know what's next or where you stand. You may also notice that your interest in people is totally different from before. Certain friendships may no longer feel aligned, or someone you never thought you'd care for suddenly becomes fascinating. This is also a transit about freedom. You might want more space from the close connections in your life and desire more time for yourself.

Remember too that this instability and quick-pivoting energy can apply to the house-specific topics that Venus rules in your personal birth chart. For example, maybe Venus is the ruler of your second house and therefore your finances, and a transit from Uranus could represent erratic ups and downs in your bank account or the need to spend a lot of money unexpectedly. Whether it's relationships, career, or creativity, when Uranus visits Venus, Venus has to approach whatever's in front of it with innovation and fresh eyes. Doing things as usual is no longer going to work.

Neptune-Venus

When Neptune and Venus interact, the rose-colored glasses are on. This transit isn't in touch with reality and can get swept away by fantasy and shiny objects. Sometimes this can get you into a tricky situation. For example, entering a relationship without fully knowing who the other person is and what their intentions are. It's easy for relational structures and boundaries to blur and disintegrate under this transit. It can be hard to tell where you end and another person begins or what you want and what another person wants. Sometimes you can be sweet-talked into something that you didn't really want to do. Try your best to enter into agreements with as much clarity as possible. Take the extra time to ask questions, make a plan, verify the dates and the details, and set boundaries and expectations before saying yes.

Neptune is like a fog, and it's easy to get a little lost on the path. This can be a welcome fog, like the fog of a new love or new creative project, or it can be a fog of grief. Neptune fully envelops you, and once its fog finally lifts, you might realize that you're very far from where you intended to go. On the other hand, this can be an exceptionally inspiring time when you feel like your creative capacity is expanding and you are open to new ideas.

Pluto-Venus

This transit can be a complete 180-degree turn for Venus. What you think is important, what you prioritize in life, and who you want to do that with may go through a top-to-bottom transformation. But remember, Venus may rule something other than relationships for you, so this transformation could be in another area. In my own life, I've experienced this as a total makeover of what I wanted and desired. For example, Venus is my career planet. I entered my Pluto-Venus transit wanting to do A, and I exited the Pluto transit wanting to do B. In order to make B happen, I had to tear A down and start from the bottom.

Connections may feel intense and all-consuming during this time. For example, you and a partner may go through a trial that seems to take up all of your personal time and space. Going down to the Pluto depths together may strengthen the bond or test its limits. Another possibility is beginning a collaboration with an influential person or entity that you never expected to be connected with. Pluto often brings up questions about power in relationships and may teach you how to stand your ground in front of someone or something that you perceive as mightier than you.

Venus Attunement and Channeling

You can do this activity with the intention of "meeting" your natal Venus, your solar return Venus, or both. I recommend doing both at different times and seeing what different messages and insights you get. For an audio version of this attunement, head to www.astrologywithclaire.com/cosmicyear.

• • • • • • •

Sit or lie down in a comfortable position. Take a deep breath, close your eyes, and settle into your body. It's a beautiful spring day, and the world is alive and fresh. You smell honeysuckle and wisteria in the air as you walk up to an ornate gate, which is covered in vines. It opens with a gentle creak, and you walk through. As you walk down the trail, your body relaxes and your mind softens. All your worries begin to melt away, and your thoughts begin to quiet. Each step moves you into a deeper state of bliss and relaxation. Your senses are heightened and enlivened. The smells are more noticeable, the colors are more saturated, the crunching of leaves and rocks beneath your feet more satisfying. Each step is an adventure in sensation. The birds sing louder and sweeter. The feel of the air on your skin is beyond pleasant—it's the perfect temperature, and you're so comfortable.

As you round a bend, the path opens into a garden in a clearing overlooking something beautiful—maybe your favorite city, maybe a valley of wildflowers, whatever's arising. There's a picnic blanket laid out in the grass with dainty plates and teacups scattered around. There are fresh-cut flowers in a vase, champagne, chocolate-covered strawberries, sandwiches, and your favorite snacks. Venus is waiting for you, sitting on the blanket, arranging the final details of your alfresco feast. You sit on a cushion next to Venus, taking a deep breath and exhaling through your mouth, completely arriving and feeling at ease here in the garden.

"Hi, love," Venus says in its honey-laced voice. "I'm so glad you're here." Take a moment to notice Venus's appearance and feel its energy. Allow Venus to take the form of a person, animal, or other being that you feel comfortable around. You can be 100 percent yourself. There's no need to strain or perform here. The ease between the two of you is unmatched. Everything in this relationship is effortless. Just being in Venus's presence further relaxes and uplifts you simultaneously. You are content, not thinking about anything else, and fully present here in the garden.

Venus pours you a glass of champagne and hands it to you. "Cheers," it says as it gently taps its glass to yours. You take a sip and exhale, sinking deeper into the cushion. Venus continues to speak in its dulcet tones. "You know you're my favorite, right? I love spending time with you. I cherish you." After a pause, Venus continues, "I hear we're going to be spending even more time together this year, and I can't tell you how excited I am. We're going to have so much fun. I was thinking we could lie back in the grass and dream about all that we want to create and do this year. What do you want more than anything?"

Pick up your pen and allow the words to flow as you answer Venus's question. Try to write uninhibited. Venus cares about everything you have to say. No desire is too silly, too small, or too large. When your writing comes to a natural end, Venus pipes in again and says, "I celebrate this list. I'm so excited about exploring these desires with you. Are you ready to hear what I'd like to add?" Once you give Venus permission, flow with it again, writing from Venus's perspective all of the pleasures, delights, and wishes Venus would like to fulfill in your life this year.

• • • • • • •

Venus Prayers

Thank you, Venus, for bringing peace and harmony to this situation.

Venus, I invite you to restore balance in this area. Thank you.

Thank you, Venus, for connecting me with those who are most supportive and beneficial for me.

Venus, I invite you to fill my heart with love. Thank you.

Thank you, Venus, for helping me see the pleasure and goodness in my life.

Venus, thank you for showering me with loving-kindness.

Thank you, Venus, for increasing my magnetism. I know that what I need and desire is on the way.

Venus, thank you for this gift. I'm available for more.

eleven

Mars

Classification: Malefic

Topics: Energy, activity, drive, conflict, war, danger, anger, competition, victory, defeat, bravery, courage, assertion, enemies, sexual intercourse

A rush of adrenaline flashes through your body. Your legs fill with blood, and your lungs fill with air. The hair on your skin stands on end. You feel electric, alive, and unstoppable. This response, whether to a threat or a thrill, is how Mars feels. The stakes are high. It's life or death. And you're ready to run. When Mars rules the energy of the year, it can feel like you're always preparing to enter the lion's den. With one emergency after another, days can feel hectic or, on the upside, exciting. Mars is always up for a challenge, and it loves to serve you plenty when it takes the reins.

Chaotic, intense, infuriating—these are a few of the ways my clients have described Mars years. Mars is one of the malefic planets, and when it's in charge, small irritations to large conflicts can pop up. But Mars isn't all bad. Depending on the position and condition of Mars in your natal chart or solar return chart, Mars years can also offer an opportunity to face your fears. There's a strong will to fight when Mars is in control, and that might mean taking power back over your life or facing something head-on that you've been afraid to look at. When Mars is activated, your willingness to push forward in life is strong.

If you have a day chart, Mars is the malefic planet from the opposite "club" or sect, which we've already identified as your most challenging planet. Yes, this might mean the upcoming year could have its fair share of bumps. The opposite-club malefic tends to bring up problems that are new or unfamiliar to you. On the other hand, the malefic planet from your same club tends to bring challenges that you know how to deal with and that you've overcome before. Although they may be annoying when they pop up again, you know what to do. When the malefic from the opposite club, in this case Mars, brings up a problem, you may not know where to begin solving it. These types of issues may feel like they've come out of nowhere. You may feel like you don't have the right tools or knowledge to address what's coming up. So if you have a day chart, and you're moving into a Mars-ruled year, it's a great idea to get a support team in place. Dealing with the malefic of the opposite club often requires outside assistance—totally doable.

If you have a night chart and Mars is your co-creator, you're probably in for an easier ride. Mars tends to wield its sword on your behalf, and although things can still get irritating and tough, you probably already know how to work with what's going to come up. Mars in a night chart tends to be excited instead of irritated, courageous instead of threatened, and assertive instead of frustrated.

What to Expect During a Mars Year

Mars is excitable and full of energy, and it reflects your level of physical energy too. I've noticed it's very common for people to take physical exercise more seriously when Mars calls the shots. But Mars is also inflaming, and it's just as common for people to report feeling blocked from exercise due to an accident, illness, or injury. Regardless, Mars's vibrant energy needs an outlet for the year to feel manageable and comfortable—if we can call Mars years comfortable.

Mars rules stress, including the stress response within your body. Mars years are a potent opportunity to really examine your stress level and tweak how you manage it. Stress is likely to be one of the dominant things you feel and making room for expressing it is paramount to your well-being at this time. Let it out, sweat it out, scream it out, walk it out, shake it out, Mars it out.

How you deal with conflict is likely to come up this year too. I'm not saying you'll be a walking magnet for disagreements, but how you assert yourself, advocate for yourself, and protect yourself and those you love is likely to be highlighted. At its best, Mars is an expert problem solver, and during a Mars year you may be obsessed with figuring out how to make something less difficult. Competition is another theme that can come up. You might feel like you're fighting for a position or promotion, or there might just be general tension in your house of the year or the natal house that holds your Mars.

Mars is sharp and it's excellent at cutting things out. When Mars is your co-creator, you may have to make some tough decisions. Instead of adding more, Mars times are often about minimizing and getting rid of things that don't work anymore. Mars excels at cutting things out and dividing things up. Use this to your advantage.

Impatience is a huge theme during Mars years. When Mars is your co-creator, you typically want things to move at breakneck speed. Mars is fast and direct and doesn't like to waste time. It knows what it wants and it wants it now. The general feeling is one of rushing. Rushing from appointment to appointment, rushing from thought to thought, rushing from one fire to the next. On the other hand, if your natal Mars or your solar return Mars is slow, retrograde, in an introverted sign or a shady house, it may not be working at the speed you want. When that happens, Mars years can feel frustrating, like you're being held up or delayed.

Befriending and expressing anger is another mainstay of a Mars year. You may notice you feel angry or irritated more than you'd prefer during this time, and depending on your chart, this may bring up all kinds of discomfort and inner dialogue about how you "shouldn't" feel this way. Anger is one of Mars's main feeling states, and it's important to acknowledge it as a friend this year. Mars years ask you to feel your anger rather than intellectualizing it. Sink into your body and feel the sensations. Try to use descriptive words—*pulsing, radiating, bursting, vibrating, burning*—and play with staying with that feeling for thirty seconds, a minute, two minutes, maybe even more as the year goes on.

I've seen plenty of blessings unfold during Mars years too. However, they tend to be laced with some type of challenge or battle. For example, I had a client fall in love during a Mars year, something they'd been desiring for a long time, only to experience some division among their friends because of this new romantic partner. That's classic Mars. The good stuff still unfolds but might come with a side of irritation. It's a mixed bag, as life usually is.

And finally, don't forget that Mars rules something very specific in your birth chart too. Check your chart for the signs of Aries and Scorpio. What houses do they occupy, and what topics do these houses represent? Managing those topics is your Mars's primary job, and when Mars is your co-creator, these themes will come to the forefront.

Reflection Questions

Explore the following questions and prompts at the beginning of your Mars co-creation cycle and reread them as time goes on.

What are you spending most of your energy on? Does this reflect the direction you truly want to go in?

Where are you spinning your wheels?

How would you like to use Mars's sharp cutting and dividing power this year?

What's your comfort level with anger? Do you welcome it or stuff it down? How can you make friends with it?

How would you feel if someone called you ambitious? Is there shame around that? What are your ambitions?

What's one fear that you'd like to face head-on this year?

If you're feeling irritated by something, what's the lesson beneath it?

Where can you be more direct about what you want or need?

Mars Tips

- Prioritize finding a physical outlet. The type and intensity are up to you.
- Come up with two or three safe and constructive ways to express your anger. Talking about it is always encouraged, but don't forget about moving it through your body. Screaming into a pillow, anyone? Visiting a rage room? If you were to make up an "anger dance," what would that choreography look like?
- Make a Mars playlist full of angsty, high-energy songs that help you feel and move with "hot" emotions.
- Get involved in causes that are important to you. Mars would love to go with you to a protest.

- Be curious about the people and activities that "inflame" you and see where you can engage with them less.
- Get really clear on how you're spending your energy and make sure you're getting a return on your investment.
- When in doubt during a Mars year, err on the side of fighting for something instead of giving up.

• • • • • • •

What About Mars Retrograde?

Mars retrograde happens about every two years and lasts a couple of months. When Mars is your co-creator, you guessed it: Mars retrograde is going to be ten times more significant for you. What I've noticed most often during Mars retrograde is a general sense of impatience and frustration. You may have been on a roll, cruising and moving forward with something, only for that something to feel like it's come to a screeching halt. Mars retrograde can feel like you're trudging through mud instead of slaying dragons left and right. This is a great opportunity to slow down and question hustle culture. Mars retrograde really prompts you to ask things like, *How much is enough? What does hard work mean to me, and do I even want to do it?*

Mars retrograde may be a time when you temporarily misdirect your efforts and energy. It'll show you very clearly where you're spinning your wheels and getting nowhere. I'll never forget one Mars retrograde when I worked really hard to obtain a certification for a career path that never worked out for me. (Hindsight: I'm glad it didn't. But as an astrologer, it's fascinating to look back and see Mars retrograde at work.)

Mars retrograde may also be a time when the focus on fighting battles and making progress reverts from outside of you to inside of you. I've noticed that Mars retrograde tends to bring up old hurts and pain that maybe you haven't addressed directly until now. Use Mars retrograde to soothe them, and you'll be sprinting by the time the retrograde is over.

Transits to Mars

While Mars is your co-creator, transits from other planets (especially slow-moving planets) to your natal Mars are primary. They're the transits most likely to correspond with the main events or turning points of your year. These transits will affect Mars's innate themes but also your Mars's personal themes based on what houses Aries and Scorpio occupy in your chart.

Moon-Mars

The Moon reflects your mood, and when it contacts Mars the mood becomes red-hot. This couple of hours can be a welcome boost of energy. On the other hand, you might notice feeling a bit more irritable or touchy when this aspect is exact. The Moon-Mars combo can be somewhat defensive at times. Giving Mars an outlet usually helps. This is a great time to do a burst of activity, whether that's work or exercise.

Mercury-Mars

Like Mars, Mercury is a quick planet; when they come together it's time to get the show on the road. It's hard to sit still under this aspect, and you may prefer to be busy or out and about. The mind and body tend to be restless and need something to do. This is an extremely dynamic combination that loves to speak its mind. You might be extra bold and spicy in your communication and may be surprised by what comes out of your mouth.

Venus-Mars

Venus brings a welcome softness to Mars's sharp edges. Venus is a planet of love, and Mars is a planet of action. Put together, this transit is like love in motion. I tend to experience this transit as one of chemistry, whether that's between you and another person or you and a creative project. Plan a date night or have a love affair with that new idea.

Sun-Mars

The Sun and Mars are both very self-assured planets, and when they're working together, they create next-level confidence. The Sun emboldens Mars and encourages it to act. On this day, you might be able to see your next steps clearly and feel brave enough to put your first foot forward. This is a pretty selfish transit, and I mean that in a good way—it's about doing what's best for you and prioritizing your agenda.

Mars-Mars

This is typically a very active couple of days. Your schedule is full, and you're motivated to get things done. Your energetic capacity is a little higher right now, so go ahead and push yourself a bit if that feels right. You have momentum and may get irritated by anyone or anything that stands in your way. You're not one to mess with right now; you mean business! Just be aware that sometimes Mars-Mars combinations can bring excess heat, manifesting as poor sleep, inflammation, agitation, or being accident-prone. I always burn myself while cooking under this transit because I tend to be moving too fast.

Jupiter-Mars

When Jupiter touches Mars, the energy is extra high. Mars's normal bravado is exaggerated under Jupiter's magnifying glass. This can show up as a welcome surge of vitality and confidence. You may feel extremely enthusiastic or fired up about something. Jupiter-Mars is like a shot of bravery and dynamism. It can also feel like a green light to move forward with something you've been wanting to do for a long time. Jupiter can bring solutions to Mars's problems, and you may finally see how you can solve something. However, on rare occasions Jupiter can just make Mars's mess bigger. The caution with Jupiter-Mars is to make sure you don't overdo it—easier said than done.

Saturn-Mars

The classic term used for this transit is *frustrating*. Saturn brings limits and obstacles to Mars's innate desire to push forward and act. Depending on the nature of the aspect, this can be experienced as a literal block or as a crucible. Regardless, it's usually an intense time of focus, hard work, and pushing yourself to your limits. Sometimes you can push too hard and move toward exhaustion. I've really begun to like Saturn-Mars interactions because they're extremely driven. If you see one of these transits coming up, plan on using its heavy striving on something important to you. Make space for a project or something you've been wanting to get done for a long time but just haven't had the *oomph* to pull off yet. Long-term Saturn-Mars transits can also feel like you're working and working and not seeing any results. This is a good time to be really strategic about how you spend your energy and restructure your commitments and priorities so that you're actually focusing on what matters most.

Uranus-Mars

This transit is somewhat similar to Jupiter-Mars but more explosive and unpredictable. When Mars is your co-creator and it's activated by Uranus, expect the unexpected. You may be working in one direction very diligently and then suddenly want to put your effort in another direction. You may find yourself doing something you didn't plan on or wouldn't normally do. This is a very electric time.

Your interest and drive may be very up and down, and your energy may come in fits and spurts. There can also be a great sense of urgency or rushing when these two planets come together. You might be faced with a decision, conflict, or idea that feels like it needs attention right away.

Neptune-Mars

Neptune is like an energy vampire. It tends to suck the life out of whatever planet it touches. When Neptune comes into contact with Mars, energy can feel like it's just pouring down the drain. Neptune-Mars is like trying to have a sword fight in a foggy field. You can't even see your opponent, but you're swinging like mad anyway, making yourself extremely tired with each blow. In real life, this might show up as sacrificing a lot of time and energy for another person or going through an arduous time that requires a lot of attention. You may feel confused about where to spend your energy and what to focus on, and this indecision can be a drain in and of itself.

Pluto-Mars

This transit is like Saturn-Mars taken up a bazillion notches. Talk about *intense*—this transit personifies the word. This is a time of extremes. You may feel like one experience is demanding all of your time and attention. It can feel like you've been taken down into the underworld to fight the battle of your life—whether that battle is getting your degree, having your first child, or going through a breakup. Whatever it is you're experiencing, you're experiencing it at a depth you never knew you could handle. On another note, this is an unstoppable combination and a very strategic time when you can be extremely laser focused. This is the energy of a specialist, not a generalist. Put all your attention into a single place and watch the power of Pluto support you.

Mars Attunement and Channeling

You can do this activity with the intention of "meeting" your natal Mars, your solar return Mars, or both. I recommend doing both at different times and seeing what different messages and insights you get. For an audio version of this attunement, head to www.astrologywithclaire.com/cosmicyear.

• • • • • • •

Sit or lie down in a comfortable position. Take a minute to settle into your body. Close your eyes, take a deep inhale through your nose, and empty it out through your mouth with an exaggerated sigh. Notice where you're holding any tension and gently invite movement and space into those areas. Adjust your posture until you feel comfortable.

Now, rub your hands together for about ten seconds, generating heat and friction. Notice the tingling, aliveness, and circulation. These are the sensations of Mars. Take a moment to invite Mars into your space, thanking it in advance for any messages and insights it has for you.

Imagine walking into a shared workshop. It's loud! Heavy metal music is blasting over the sounds of drills and saws, and sparks are flying everywhere. The smell of gas and oil is heavy, and it's so hot that a little sweat begins to form on your back.

You spot Mars in the back fixing up an old car. You'd recognize those red, scuffed-up work boots anywhere. You just observe Mars in its element for a while. It's full of life and power. It knows exactly what it's doing and doesn't have an ounce of insecurity. It's masterful.

As you make your way around piles of scrap metal and wood, Mars turns and gives you an inviting wave. There's a dinged-up couch in the corner that Mars motions you toward. It's got a few grease stains, but it welcomes you in, squishy and comfortable.

"What's up?" Mars says as it heads over to a mini fridge to get itself a beer. It kicks off its boots and sinks in next to you with a big exhale. "I hear we're stuck together this year," it says with a chuckle and an elbow into your side. "Just kidding. I've been looking forward to seeing you." Mars takes a sip and then continues, "I've actually scribbled down some priorities, things that I want to help you do this year. I'm ready for you to put me to work, boss." Mars reaches into its pocket and pulls out a crumpled piece of coffee-stained paper. It has three priorities listed on it. What are they?

Free write on these three items until you feel complete. Feel free to ask Mars clarifying questions or to even push back if you have different ideas. If you get stuck, simply describe Mars's appearance and the workshop that you're in until something comes through.

• • • • • • •

Mars Prayers

Thank you, Mars, for filling my body with energy.

Mars, I invite you to show me how to advocate for myself in this situation. Thank you.

Thank you, Mars, for filling me with strength and power.

Mars, I invite you to show me what needs to be eliminated or cut out. Thank you.

Thank you, Mars, for filling me with courage.

Mars, I invite you to go before me with your sword of protection. Thank you.

Thank you, Mars, for showing me the perfect strategy.

Mars, I invite you to make me victorious in this situation. Thank you.

Thank you, Mars, for giving me the confidence to take the first step.

twelve

Jupiter

Classification: Benefic

Topics: Expansion, growth, children, elevation, wisdom, freedom, favor, spirituality, accumulation, abundance, wealth

Your phone dings as you come in from a leisurely walk in the sunshine. It's an email. *What?* You pause to read it a second time. *Really?* It's from someone you haven't heard from in so long, you assumed the connection had come to a natural end. They have a big opportunity and thought of you. *Me?* The best part is, you've already been thinking about this idea. It's like the person read your mind or the Universe is giving you a big wink: *You're on the right path.* A smile breaks across your face, and your whole body lights up with a feeling of *yes!* This is just a small taste of what a Jupiter time may bring.

I'm in a Jupiter year right now as I type this. No, I haven't won the lottery . . . yet. But I was gifted a used car, asked to write this book, and received a few other unexpected invitations that lit me up. I'd say that's pretty awesome. Jupiter opens doors. How big those doors are depends on the context, but expect to walk across a few thresholds.

If you have a day chart, Jupiter is the planet willing and able to do the most good for you. And so, a Jupiter year may be one of the more life-affirming years you can experience. If you have a night chart, goodness still prevails, but it may be on a smaller scale than a Venus year—the planet that has the most juice for you. Like all years, Jupiter years are layered, but the general undertone is one of benefit and growth.

What to Expect During a Jupiter Year

Jupiter seasons are about more, and when it's switched on, you might feel like you generally want more out of life. It's a time of envisioning something better and beginning to reach for that vision. Jupiter seeks to upgrade and improve whatever it rules in your chart, whether that's your home, relationships, or health. (Hint: What houses do Sagittarius and Pisces occupy?) Jupiter years are about hope. Jupiter says, "This is good, but it could be great," and prompts you to take the next step up the ladder of fulfillment.

Jupiter times are also about growth. This could manifest as many different types of growth—personal growth, career growth, relational growth, spiritual growth, financial growth—it really depends on where Jupiter is in your chart and what it rules. But generally, Jupiter expands and increases whatever it touches. It upsizes. It might expand so much that you actually grow out of something, which could show up as a natural (and usually amicable) end to an experience or relationship.

Jupiter will stretch you. Like I said earlier, Jupiter opens doors and brings opportunities, but you are the one who has to say yes and step through. Don't be surprised if Jupiter brings something that requires a little courage. A few growing pains are possible. Regardless, err on the side of saying yes during a Jupiter time. Jupiter is extremely enthusiastic and willing to sign up for anything. Take that risk, try something new, and trust that whatever's presenting is in your best interest.

Jupiter is a planet of freedom, and when Jupiter is activated, you too might desire to be untethered. Jupiter wants to make its own decisions and do its own thing. It wants the freedom and autonomy to explore the world and gather wisdom from all its corners. When Jupiter is tied down or understimulated, you might feel restless and itchy. If you're constantly saying no to yourself and your desire to explore and expand, a Jupiter year could actually be uncomfortable.

Imagine Jupiter as a hot-air balloon, and you're riding in the basket. Jupiter brings you up, up, up to a high and elevated place. In real life, this might look like receiving more recognition or respect at work or among friends. It could look like hitting a high point in your career or personal life. Promotions are common during Jupiter years, as are just general improvements in status and positive financial bumps. On another note, it could also look like being regarded as someone with keen insight and perspective.

Jupiter is a planet of wisdom and learning. I can't tell you how many courses I bought during my recent Jupiter year, but it's an embarrassing amount. Jupiter simply can't know enough and wants to learn things from a lot of different people and perspectives. It would also love to be regarded as an expert in its field. I encourage you to do some type of learning enrichment this year, whether for work or pleasure. I've also noticed a theme of people transitioning from student to teacher during a Jupiter time—see if that resonates with you.

Jupiter is an answer seeker. It's a spiritually driven planet, and when it's your co-creator, you often want to understand how the world works and your place within it. You may find yourself searching for meaning and asking hard questions like *What's my purpose? Why am I here? What's the greater meaning of my life?* To answer these questions, you might be drawn to Jupiter topics like religion, spirituality, or philosophy.

And finally, don't forget that Jupiter rules something very specific in your birth chart too. Check your chart for the signs of Sagittarius and Pisces. What houses do they occupy, and what topics do these houses represent? Managing those topics is your Jupiter's primary job, and when Jupiter is your co-creator, these themes will come to the forefront.

• • • • • • •

Reflection Questions

Explore the following questions and prompts at the beginning of your Jupiter co-creation cycle and reread them as time goes on.

What's my definition of abundance? How does abundance feel in my body?

Where would I like to stretch myself and reach for more this year?

What's an area of life I'd like to upgrade, and how can I begin doing that?

If I had complete freedom, I would . . .

If money weren't an object, I would . . .

What would I like to learn this year and who or what will help me on that path?

I'm ready to teach . . .

Where do I need a perspective shift, and what things or practices will help me shift it?

Jupiter Tips

- Make a Jupiter wish list. Be free and wild with it. Nothing is too big for Jupiter!
- Play with saying yes more than you say no this year. Be willing to take a risk and try something new.
- Begin a spiritual practice or strengthen one you already have.

- Find a mentor or be a mentor to someone else.
- Try to take a thirty-thousand-foot view of all things. Zoom out and gain some perspective before choosing.
- If possible, get out of your normal environment and learn about and experience a different culture.
- Pick up a few books on philosophy or spirituality.
- Set aside part of your budget for education this year. You're going to want it!
- Lean into lightheartedness and generosity as guiding principles this year.
- Have something to share? Organize a class and celebrate yourself as a teacher.

• • • • • • •

What About Jupiter Retrograde?

Jupiter retrograde happens every year and lasts about four months. When Jupiter is your co-creator, its retrograde cycle creates two important bookends for you: the moment it stations retrograde and the moment it stations direct. You might notice that you make important decisions or have shifts in focus during the weeks surrounding these exact times. Retrogrades are simply changes in direction, and you might mirror this by temporarily changing direction too.

I think it's really important to rebrand retrogrades and make sure you're not afraid of them. They're not "bad"; they're just different. Jupiter is simply operating in an alternative way than usual. It has new priorities when it's retrograde compared to when it's direct. I like to think of a retrograde as a planet taking a rest or a back seat. It's a time of renewal. If Jupiter is your co-creator, try to go with the flow and enjoy the more leisurely pace while it's retrograde. If there's a slowdown or pause in your momentum and enthusiasm, remember it's temporary and that it'll return tenfold. Some astrologers like to make the distinction that Jupiter retrograde is about internal growth, while Jupiter in direct motion is more about external growth. See if that resonates with you.

Classic retrograde words like *reviewing, redoing, revising, recalibrating,* and *revisiting* apply to Jupiter retrograde, but so do *detours, delays,* and *distractions.* A four-month distraction sounds like a long time, but I like to believe that cosmic time isn't human time and that Jupiter can make up for any "lost" time in a single second. "Nothing is lost or wasted" is a great Jupiter mindset. Jupiter thinks everything is a growth opportunity, including that tangent you took.

During one of my Jupiter years, I started studying something very intensely near the beginning of its retrograde. I worked really hard on this project, and it consumed all of my attention. But when the retrograde ended, not only was I done focusing on that thing, that thing ended up not working out for me. But here's the Jupiter part: Something new and better did. Now, this will not be the story for all Jupiter retrogrades. You won't get distracted and "waste" all your energy. But my point is, even with a temporary lapse in better judgment, Jupiter pulled through for me. It still had something delightful to offer.

Jupiter, How Does Your Garden Grow?

Another thing to pay attention to during a Jupiter year is what sign or signs it's moving through. Jupiter takes roughly one year to move through one zodiac sign, which means that depending on when you were born, Jupiter will probably straddle two signs in your profection year. Take a minute to think about the differences between these two expressions of Jupiter. How does its growth style change? How might it accumulate differently in this sign versus the next one?

Jupiter in Fire signs (Aries, Leo, Sagittarius): Grows by messing around, trying something out, and taking risks.

Jupiter in Earth signs (Taurus, Virgo, Capricorn): Grows by pruning. This version of Jupiter does more by doing less more efficiently.

Jupiter in Air signs (Gemini, Libra, Aquarius): Grows by making social connections and joining groups.

Jupiter in Water signs (Cancer, Scorpio, Pisces): Grows intuitively and is led to its next step by relying on Spirit. Grows by doing what feels comforting and safe. (This is countercultural!)

Special Conditions of Jupiter

It's always a good idea to check if Jupiter will be in an "extreme" environment while it's your co-creator. If Jupiter is in one of the signs below in either your natal chart or your solar return chart, the events of the year may be a bit more pronounced.

Jupiter in Gemini and Virgo

This Jupiter can be a little scattered and have its hands in a lot of pots. Occasionally, the outcome of this is spreading yourself too thin and not seeing the growth that you wanted because you diluted your focus in so many directions. Sometimes I've also seen this show up as opportunities with qualifiers. For example, you get a promotion, but you don't love the job. Or you receive an offer, but it's not as big as you hoped. The gift is still there, but it's not quite 100 percent. Jupiter in detriment is also about growing in an alternative way and choosing the unorthodox path. You may decide to go in a direction that's unexpected or different from your norm, and that's okay!

Jupiter in Capricorn (Fall)

When Jupiter has "fallen" to a lower place, it has a hard time elevating you. Remember that Jupiter is a free spirit, and it wants to be uninhibited. But when Jupiter is in Capricorn, it's in Saturn's house and it has to play by Saturn's rules. Jupiter in Capricorn can feel very limited by Saturn's tight structure. This might mean having to be more measured about the opportunities you take or having to be more responsible about the way you move forward. Sometimes Jupiter in Capricorn is about saying no and cutting back in order to say yes to something else.

Jupiter in Cancer (Exaltation)

A planet that's exalted is like being someone's honored guest. You get to sit at the head of the table, you get double the dessert, *and* you get presents! When Jupiter is in the Moon's sign, things are fertile and ready to grow. This is a great time to plant seeds that you want to nurture for a very long time. This version of Jupiter is about togetherness and bonding, and with it, you can make "sticky" alliances and connections with people that are able to encourage and lift you up. These are win-win situations. An exalted Jupiter may also bring you honors and recognition or put you in the right place at the right time.

Jupiter in Sagittarius and Pisces (Rulership/Domicile)

This is the most unrestrained and empowered Jupiter you can have. Jupiter is "at home" and has all its favorite things on hand, which means you have access to everything you need to succeed this year. When natal Jupiter or solar return Jupiter are in Sagittarius or Pisces, you can expect the best Jupiter has to offer with regard to the topics it manages in your chart. This might also look like you really taking charge in your life, believing that you deserve better, and taking the next steps to make it happen.

Transits to Jupiter

While Jupiter is your co-creator, transits from other planets (especially slow-moving planets) to your natal Jupiter are primary. They're the transits most likely to correspond with the main events or turning points of your year. These transits will affect Jupiter's innate themes but also your Jupiter's personal themes based on what houses Sagittarius and Pisces occupy in your chart.

Moon-Jupiter

This can be a fun few hours. The Moon amplifies Jupiter's good cheer and tends to flavor the moment with hope and optimism. Things feel brighter and even hard things seem possible. This is a generally warm and gregarious aspect and tends to be a good time for socializing and having fun.

Mercury-Jupiter

This is a fantastic transit for learning something new or for sharing knowledge. Mercury is the planet of communication and information, and Jupiter is the planet of wisdom and dissemination. Together, they love snuggling up with a good book or digging into a course. This is also prime time for sharing news or content that you want to have a broad reach. In my own life, I love this short transit for batch-creating or writing large amounts of material.

Venus-Jupiter

A Venus-Jupiter combination can't be beaten. This is some of the best cosmic weather you can ask for. When the two benefic planets are working together, the brighter events of your year are more likely to unfold. Life feels sweet and hopes are high. Keep your eyes peeled for Venus dressed up as a helpful person or a new opportunity. Enter into this day intentionally looking for what's working in your life and let yourself enjoy it. And if something new comes your way, flirt with saying yes—it might end up being one of the best decisions you've made all year.

Sun-Jupiter

Grab your sunnies! The two planets with the brightest outlook are holding hands today. This transit brings a boost in confidence. It can also elevate you to a position of leadership or increased favor. There's a spiritual side to this transit too. In ancient astrology, the Sun represents the divine. When it touches Jupiter, the planet of insight, you might have increased access to divine wisdom and knowledge. Set aside some time for spiritual practice. Pull some cards, do a ritual, pray, or grab your journal and connect with the divine within and around you.

Mars-Jupiter

I imagine this transit as a revving engine. When these two enthusiastic planets come together, you might feel unstoppable. Mars lights a fire under Jupiter's big ideas and says, "Go!" There are a few cautions, however. Sometimes Mars makes Jupiter a bit arrogant, as if there's only one way to do something. This combo can get a little preachy. Other times, Mars encourages Jupiter to bite off more than it can chew. This might look like saying yes to multiple commitments only to realize you don't actually have the bandwidth to satisfy them all.

Jupiter-Jupiter

If Jupiter is your co-creator, and it receives a transit from real-time Jupiter, pay attention! Although not always super obvious, this is likely to coincide with a turn of events, usually for the better. For example, when this happened to me, my husband and I made a decision to move. When your co-creator is activated in a significant way, you may be making pivotal decisions about your general life direction.

Jupiter-Jupiter transits also tend to bring up your beliefs and the concept of faith. Depending on the rest of the astrological context, this might actually show up as a crisis of belief. I'll never forget one Jupiter return that happened while I was writing my first book. It coincided with me questioning everything I believed about wellness (pretty hard when you're writing a wellness book). It was really disruptive at the time, but essential for my growth and life direction—things that Jupiter fosters. Questions to ask when Jupiter touches Jupiter include *Do I really believe this? Have I outgrown this? Can I reach for something better?*

Saturn-Jupiter

Saturn-Jupiter is an interesting transit. We have two planets that represent opposite forces coming together and engaging. One planet wants more; one planet wants less. One planet represents expansion and the other contraction. There are a lot of astrology details that determine which one wins out, but regardless, the lesson tends to be the same: learning to grow in a way that's sustainable and measured. This is a fantastic transit for long-term planning and getting serious about what you want. It forces the Jupiter dream down to Earth. Saturn cools Jupiter off and mellows it out. Occasionally this can feel like a buzzkill, but I believe it's in Jupiter's best interest. Think of this transit as a refining or maturing of Jupiter's vision and enthusiasm. When you can get a handle on this transit, you can create something that lasts for a long time, whether it's a business or a partnership.

Uranus-Jupiter

Buckle up! This transit is fire. These planets share a desire to have peak experiences and grow at an exponential rate. Together they can be a wild ride. Jupiter is already uninhibited, and Uranus gives it even more juice. Things can progress at an unbelievably rapid pace.

For example, a new opportunity may present itself to you, but it comes with a side of overwhelm due to the size or the speed. You may notice that you want to say yes to everything, and maybe you can, but just be aware that there's also a high risk of burnout and overextension with these two planets. This is definitely a transit that defines taking a risk. Depending on the rest of the astrological context, this may be the perfect time to go for it, whatever it is. Just expect the road ahead to be anything but stable. It's going to have extreme ups and downs and a lot of twists and turns, but it'll be anything but boring.

Neptune-Jupiter

The Neptune-Jupiter transit can create a bit of a confused Jupiter. On the one hand, dreams that you've had for a really long time may come to pass. It might feel a bit like a fairytale. On the other hand, it can be really hard for Jupiter to get motivated and to get going. Neptune is a fatiguing force. Neptune's also like a smoke machine, covering the dance floor so you can't see who you're swaying with. When Jupiter and Neptune are in contact, it's always a great idea to draw yourself a map. Where do you want to go, and how are you going to get there? With Neptune in the mix, you can plan for distractions and maybe getting lost a few times. You can get there in the end; you just might need a few reminders of where you're headed. I like to encourage clients experiencing this transit to get objective guidance and outside support when making decisions. You might not have the clearest vision at this time, and it can be really helpful to get a second set of eyes on the situation.

Pluto-Jupiter

Pluto-Jupiter is a power-hungry Jupiter. Pluto represents control, and Jupiter represents growth. When these two planets interact, you might notice an extreme growth spurt in the amount of sway and responsibility you have in your life. This transit tends to come with a good amount of success and advancement. Suddenly, you realize how much influence you have, or occasionally, that someone else has. This aspect can feel weighty, like you're carrying so much on your shoulders. This is also a wisdom-bestowing transit. Jupiter desires to understand, and Pluto is obsessed with the truth. In combination, you might feel like a super-seeker, where you're getting to the bottom of something, investigating the mysteries of life, and redefining your beliefs.

Jupiter Attunement and Channeling

You can do this activity with the intention of "meeting" your natal Jupiter, your solar return Jupiter, or both. I recommend doing both at different times and seeing what different messages and insights you get. For an audio version of this attunement, head to www.astrologywithclaire.com/cosmicyear.

• • • • • • •

Sit or lie down in a comfortable position. Take a moment to settle into your body. Close your eyes and begin to deepen your breath. Notice how your breath not only fills your belly and chest but the back of your body too. Feel your whole torso inflate like a balloon as you exaggerate the inhales. This sensation of filling and inflating belongs to Jupiter. Invite Jupiter into your space and thank it for the wisdom it's about to share with you.

Imagine you're at the airport. You have your ticket and your passport, and you've made it through security with no hiccups. Your travel outfit is on point, and you're feeling quite chic. You walk briskly through the terminal and have just enough time for an espresso before boarding—perfection.

You board the plane, and as you get closer to your row you see Jupiter in the seat next to yours. You promised to meet each other here when the time was right, and that time is now. As you walk down the aisle, you notice Jupiter's T-shirt says "Wander" in big block letters, and it's reading a travel guide on your destination. Its water bottle is covered in stickers from shops and cafés all around the world, and it frequently looks up from its book to crack jokes with the passengers around it. Jupiter is infectious and has already made friends.

You have a smooth takeoff and make it to cruising altitude. You snuggle into your window seat and enjoy the thirty-thousand-foot view. "Beautiful, isn't it?" Jupiter gently interrupts. "I've got to say, I'm so excited about going on this trip with you. We're going to experience some incredible things together. You know, being this high up really helps my perspective. It's like I can finally see how everything fits together. Speaking of, do you have any paper? I want to draw you a map of where we're going this year."

You pull out your journal, and Jupiter begins to sketch. Allow Jupiter to take over your pen and just go with the flow. Draw a map of the year ahead. Where are you two going? And what do you need to take with you? If you get to the point where you want to write longhand, feel free. This is your practice and there's no wrong way to do it.

• • • • • • •

Jupiter Prayers

Thank you, Jupiter, for filling my heart with hope.

Jupiter, I invite you to show me what's working here. Thank you.

Thank you, Jupiter, for giving me a fresh perspective here.

Jupiter, I invite you to bring me new opportunities and invitations. Thank you.

Thank you, Jupiter, for elevating me and allowing me to succeed.

Jupiter, thank you for providing everything I need and more.

Thank you, Jupiter, for connecting me with the wisdom and teachers who are most beneficial for me.

Jupiter, I invite you to bring even more goodness to this situation. Show me what you've got. Thank you.

thirteen

Saturn

Classification: Malefic

Topics: Isolation, separation, hardship, suffering, structure, order, endurance, responsibility, limitations, maturity, elders, father

Your alarm goes off at 5:00 a.m. You put on your slippers and head to your desk, putting the kettle on along the way. While the water boils, you open your laptop and begin typing. You pick up your project right where you left off. When the world is asleep, you shine. Word by word, morning by morning, you're building the future you want. It's not easy. It's not fun. Sometimes you can't believe you've got to wake up and do it all over again. But you're determined to get the work done.

Saturn is a hard, dry force that brings about things that are heavy, dense, tedious, and long-suffering. When Saturn rules the times, it may present something that at first feels impossible. *How am I going to do this?* You try to resist the challenge or to go around it, but you soon realize there's no other option but to go straight through. And you do. And you survive. If you allow it, this is the type of fortitude and resolve a Saturn season can build within you.

A Saturn year may feel more constructive or destructive depending on the club (a.k.a. sect) of your chart. Saturn is part of the day club, and because of that, it tends to build things up in a day chart and deconstruct things in a night chart. Just like Mars years are especially spicy for day charts, Saturn years may be a little more strenuous for night charts. But despite the heaviness and the seriousness, I've got to be honest, Saturn might be my favorite planet, and if you flipped here first, you have a special place in my heart. Without Saturn, you wouldn't build things that endure or establish structures for your life to blossom within. Saturn helps you create forms that you're proud of and that mature you into who you want to be. If you can get through a Saturn year, you can get through anything.

What to Expect During a Saturn Year

When Saturn is your co-creator, the foundation of your life tends to take center stage. It may be a time of "kicking the tires" to make sure they're still good and assessing the supports in your life to see if they're really giving you what you need. Saturn loves to pour a strong foundation, but it's equally possible for something foundational in your life to feel a bit rocky or to even disintegrate when Saturn comes to town. Saturn giveth and Saturn taketh away. If something isn't strong enough, deep enough, or high-quality enough to support you for years to come, it's unlikely to survive a Saturn year. This is good news! Saturn clears a path so that something better and more supportive can be built. You may not understand what Saturn's doing in the moment, but it tends to make all the sense in the world when you look back.

Saturn times are often about the essentials and necessities. This planet is all business. Frivolity and fun (What's fun?!) tend to be a bit out of reach. It's common for Saturn to demand you put aside the pleasurable things for the responsible things, at least for a moment. Saturn rewards hard work and when it rules your calendar, you often find yourself with your nose in a book or clocking in at work for overtime. Saturn demands a lot from you—a lot of energy, focus, determination, and commitment.

During a recent Saturn year, I was pushed to my breaking point and decided to take some time away to regroup and get back to the basics. I put astrology on pause and got a job in my local community. I spent time just focusing on being somewhere consistently and paying the bills without the roller coaster of entrepreneurship. Although it didn't last forever, and it wasn't my favorite thing in the world, it was something that felt nourishing to my nervous system at the time. Saturn years are often about doing what's best for right now, even if that thing isn't the shiniest or the sexiest. Trust that something better is being knit together below your feet, even if you can't see it yet. Stay the course.

Saturn times may also bring about some loneliness. This might be because you're working long hours and don't have the time or energy to see your friends, or you might be secluded for another reason like illness or a move. Sometimes you're physically distanced from the people you love due to a work assignment. Regardless, Saturn loves its alone time and encourages ample turning inward and reflecting.

If you are spending time with loved ones and friends, you might notice the need to erect new boundaries in your relationships. Saturn likes to keep things separate, distinct, and clear, and it's also skilled at saying no thank you. There may be a relationship that desperately needs some limits or some maturing. Saturn often facilitates this by bringing you through a trying time together. This gives the relationship an opportunity to either deepen or to show its cracks, and it's up to you to decide if you stay or go.

A Saturn year is perfect for buckling down and focusing. It has a unique way of simplifying things, melting distractions away, and leaving only the most essential priority behind. If Saturn hasn't already picked for you, choose something that you want to master and create a plan to do so. Saturn adores time management and organization, and you might find that all things efficiency become fascinating. Whether it's classic time blocking or an alternative calendaring system, like working with the Moon or the menstrual cycle, explore new ways to focus and organize your time.

As the planet of consistency and long-term effort, it's no surprise that Saturn rules two years in a row. How lucky. You don't just get one year of playing by the rules, redefining your life's supports, and pushing yourself to your limit; you get two. From what I've noticed in practice, the second year tends to be a little bit easier. Now, there are a lot of astrological caveats to this, but what's also true is that once you live through something, you inevitably gain tools and perspectives that you didn't have before. You get to bypass that learning curve during the second Saturn year and move straight into the work. Saturn is the only planet with this unique double feature.

• • • • • • •

Reflection Questions

Explore the following questions and prompts at the beginning of your Saturn co-creation cycle and reread them as time goes on.

What would I like to build with Saturn over the next two years?

Where would I like to put more steady effort and consistent attention?

Where do I feel unsupported and what can I do to support myself?

What structures in my life are ready to be torn down and rebuilt?

What in my life would benefit from more discipline? What does this look like to me practically?

What needs to be broken down into more manageable pieces so that I can approach it with more consistency and less dread?

What in my life would benefit from more boundaries and more structure? How can I begin to incorporate this today?

If I could only produce or do one thing with excellence for the next two years, what would that thing be? What's the most important priority this year?

What do I need to say no to this year in order to say yes to the thing I listed above?

If everything in my life melted away—my identity, my possessions, my relationships, my career, my titles—what's left at the foundation? How can I strengthen this?

Saturn Tips

- Saturn says no, not yet, or not like that. During a Saturn year, err on the side of saying no, especially to things that aren't a full-body yes. Less is more when Saturn's in charge.
- Finally organize your desk and use Saturn to get all your paperwork in order.
- Ready for an eye-opening experience? Try doing a time audit. For three days (or a whole week if you're feeling serious), track how much time you spend doing each activity. Then comb through the data and see where you can make things more efficient.
- Give yourself permission to really geek out on calendaring this year. Try different methods of organizing your day and see what feels the best.

- Don't have a five-year plan? This is the year to make one.
- Pick up a book on the art of setting boundaries at work and in relationships.
- Saturn supports structures, including your body's hard structures and boundaries. Give some TLC to your skin, nails, bones, and joints this year.
- Saturn loves heavy things. If it calls to you, try picking up weight training this year.
- Make a list of "Saturn supports"—people, practices, or things that make you feel grounded. If you ever feel shaky, check your list and pick something to do or someone to reach out to.
- Take a long-term view of every decision. Try to think about what makes the most sense for years to come instead of what makes sense for right now.

What About Saturn Retrograde?

Saturn retrograde occurs once per year and lasts approximately four and a half months. No matter what planet is retrograde, putting *re-* in front of its keywords is helpful. With Saturn, you might spend these months restructuring, reorganizing, reestablishing, reaffirming, and refocusing.

When Saturn stations retrograde, its plodding, consistent pace tends to morph into a slog, and the things it normally does with ease take a little more time and effort. Saturn retrograde may bring some delays or detours to your year. You may feel like you get distracted or that there's suddenly a roadblock that wasn't there before. This is often a time of creative problem-solving and learning how to either get around what's popped up or surrender and work with whatever's in front of you.

Saturn is about clarity and precision and that tends to be even more the case when it's retrograde. Its capacity to do is lessened, and it is more interested in doing one thing exceptionally well. You may spend these months working very intently on one project or addressing one consistent problem.

Transits to Saturn

While Saturn is your co-creator, transits from other planets (especially slow-moving planets) to your natal Saturn are primary. They're the transits most likely to correspond with the main events or turning points of your year. These transits will affect Saturn's innate themes but also your Saturn's personal themes based on what houses Capricorn and Aquarius occupy in your chart.

Moon-Saturn

During the handful of hours that the Moon transits Saturn, it's easy to feel a little glass half empty. Try not to take yourself or your feelings too seriously and know that the Moon moves quickly and will soon leave Saturn behind. You might desire some alone time or feel more inward than usual. Like most activations of Saturn, this is a good time to focus your energy on something specific and practical.

Mercury-Saturn

This day is really great for sorting out the details. Plan to make a plan. Get your dates in order, write out your to-do lists and major goals, or get your paperwork organized. Mercury loves the minutiae, and Saturn lives to simplify. When together, they love to edit and refine things. When Mercury comes to Saturn, the mental atmosphere can be a bit serious or even somewhat down. Keep in mind, this is just a short transit and having a project to focus on usually helps pep you up.

Venus-Saturn

When Venus and Saturn interact there can be some tension between what you want to do and what you feel like you "have" to do. Venus is all about play, and Saturn is all about business, and they don't often mix smoothly. You might be more perceptive of relationships or things in your life that feel unsupportive or disappointing. This short transit has loner vibes, and it's easy to feel ignored or isolated. Instead of getting down in the dumps, intentionally plan to spend this time nurturing the bond with yourself—the most long-term (Saturn) relationship (Venus) you have.

Sun-Saturn

I like to view the Sun-Saturn transit as a reality check. The Sun brings its spotlight to the planet that represents objectivity, making it easier to see what's been accomplished and what's still outstanding. Sun-Saturn combinations can feel a bit like getting graded. It's tempting to be too hard on yourself and feel like you're not meeting your own expectations. Remember that you're enough, and you're doing the best you can! The Sun also brings some brightness to Saturn's dark corners. Allow the Sun to shine its light on Saturn's shadows and try to just stay curious. What fears are here? What tenderness is here?

Mars-Saturn

Depending on the type of aspect Mars makes to Saturn, this can be a supercharged or a frustrating couple of days. I tend to experience it as a mix. Both planets like to get things done, and in combination, there's often an urgency to bust through a block or to accomplish something massive. The only issue is that Mars likes to rush, and Saturn prefers a slow and measured pace. This clash can create some irritation or a choppy feeling of one step forward, two steps back. This is a great time to reassess any long-term goals and plans and make sure they still feel correct for you. Mars might show you where a system, plan, or commitment is inefficient. Use this transit and any annoyance that pops up as guides to help you simplify and align your efforts. What's absolutely essential?

Jupiter-Saturn

Jupiter tends to challenge Saturn's limits and restrictions and encourages you to break free. This transit often brings a lot of restlessness. If you've been feeling constrained or stuck, Jupiter's influence may bring not only the desire but the energy and courage to make a change. You might make some very significant shifts to the underlying structures of your life during this transit in the name of freedom. If you're not feeling stuck, this transit can be extremely productive, like a cosmic growth spurt. You can use Jupiter and Saturn to build upon the successful structures that you already have in place, reinforcing them and ensuring that they last for a very long time.

Saturn-Saturn

You know the saying "between a rock and a hard place"? That's a good description of a Saturn-Saturn combination. Occasionally, these times may feel like you're pushing and pushing and pushing, but nothing seems to be panning out. You may not see the benefit or the result that you were hoping for, and you have to stop, reassess, and go back to the foundation and try again. But there's another side to these transits. They're like thresholds of maturity. I've experienced them as a pressure cooker and a call to step up and meet a challenge. You might doubt that you have what it takes to overcome it, but no matter what, you have to address it—there's no other way around. Saturn-Saturn gives you the opportunity to come into your own version of excellence, if you're willing to put in the work. For example, my most recent Saturn-Saturn combination correlated with a really challenging time at work. I was pressed to do things that stretched me and made me uncomfortable. I felt like I was being tested and asked to put my skills to use in a higher-stakes way than ever before. However, despite the discomfort, all of those things strengthened my foundation and made me a more confident astrologer.

Uranus-Saturn

The Uranus-Saturn transit is a clash of opposites. Saturn is a buttoned-up planet that respects rules and regulations, while Uranus couldn't care less about them. When Uranus comes to Saturn, it can really rock the foundation of your life, if not totally break it apart. This may be an exciting or tumultuous time when the fabric of your life is being redefined. Everything from your day-to-day routine to your relationships and how you put food on the table can feel up in the air. Things that have always felt solid may suddenly feel unstable, and things that were once nonnegotiable suddenly feel negotiable. This combination can really open you up to a new reality. When Uranus touches Saturn, there can be an urgent feeling of wanting to break out of anything that's constricting you or anything that feels out of alignment with your authentic nature. This urgent energy can be used to pop you out of a long-term rut or unhelpful pattern. It may feel unbalanced at the time, but it can be very liberating if you don't cling and allow Uranus to do its work. Take the leap.

Neptune-Saturn

Neptune also erodes Saturn's boundaries, but it does so in a totally different way from Uranus. Neptune tends to be less shocking and more gradual. Neptune's waves lap at Saturn's shores and gently eat away at them until they can't be stood upon. Neptune will show you where Saturn's seemingly solid structures or supports are actually weak. During this transit, you may realize that something you relied on isn't what it seems, that things aren't as secure as you hoped, and that everything eventually washes away. There's also an opportunity here to let go, to surrender what's not working, and to dream about what could be. This transit is also a story about fantasy versus reality. When Neptune and Saturn interact, it can be really hard to tell what's real and what's an illusion. It's always a great idea to get outside support and guidance during a Neptune transit if you feel unclear.

Pluto-Saturn

Pluto tends to change things so dramatically that they're unrecognizable. Although a bit tired and maybe a tad cheesy, the metaphor of the transition from caterpillar to butterfly is exactly the type of shift that Pluto brings. When it touches Saturn, Pluto takes Saturn things like structure, foundations, and reality down to the underworld and returns them to you in a shape that you never expected. These are the "never the same since" experiences. Similar to Uranus but a bit more foundational and long-lasting, Pluto transits to Saturn indicate a life-altering restructuring of your reality—a big transition where life was one way and now it's another way. These are years that you remember, that you point back to and say, "Oh, that was when everything changed."

Saturn Attunement and Channeling

You can do this activity with the intention of "meeting" your natal Saturn, your solar return Saturn, or both. I recommend doing both at different times and seeing what different messages and insights you get. For an audio version of this attunement, head to www.astrologywithclaire.com/cosmicyear.

• • • • • • •

Sit or lie down in a comfortable position. Take a few moments to notice the structures supporting your body—the furniture, the floor, the ground beneath you. With each breath, see if you can sink deeper into these structures, allowing them to hold you. You don't have to do all the work.

When you feel ready, bring your attention to your skin—one of the many boundaries Saturn rules. Notice the tingling and aliveness at the skin layer, and how your skin is both the barrier and the communicator between you and the outside world. Then slowly sink your attention through the fascia and muscle until you arrive at the bone layer. This is the realm of Saturn. Take a few moments to hang out here, gently sinking back to the bone layer when your mind drifts up.

Now, imagine walking down a long flight of stairs, eventually arriving in a basement. The basement can look any way you like. Take a few moments to notice the light, the smells, and the furnishings.

Then make your way over to a wall, pressing a button that opens a secret passageway. As you walk through the passageway it begins to broaden, opening into a larger hallway. It may remind you of a university, library, or another place of study. Walk past many office doors until you reach the end of the hall. "Saturn," the placard on the last door says. Open the door and walk in.

First, take a moment to notice the room. What's the furniture like? The artwork? The overall design? If there's music playing, what is it? Now, notice that Saturn is here. Saturn looks like you, just older. Notice what Saturn's wearing, how its hair is styled, how it looks at you. How do you feel in this wise Saturn's presence?

Saturn invites you to sit at a desk while it stands in front of an old-fashioned blackboard. "Welcome to my office," Saturn says. "It takes some grit to find me, but you did it." Saturn takes a sip of black coffee and continues, "I hear we're going to be spending quite a bit of time together. I have a plan for how I'd like to spend the upcoming months. I also have some insight into what's working and what's not working in your life. Are you ready?"

After you give Saturn permission to share, it grabs a piece of chalk, turns to the blackboard, and begins to write a bulleted list. Write down the title of the list and just let the words flow from here. Remember, if you get stuck, you can always return to describing the scene or Saturn's appearance.

• • • • • • •

Saturn Prayers

Thank you, Saturn, for supporting me.

Saturn, I invite you to restructure this for me. Thank you.

Thank you, Saturn, for strengthening me and building me up.

Saturn, I invite you to give me the wisdom to handle this situation maturely. Thank you.

Thank you, Saturn, for giving me the discipline and focus to bring this to completion.

Saturn, I invite you to show me how to overcome this obstacle. Thank you.

Thank you, Saturn, for helping me make something that will stand the test of time.

Saturn, I invite you to provide all the practical supports I need to live my life. Thank you.

Thank you, Saturn, for moving me into my excellence and most established self.

fourteen

The Birthday Ritual

Exploring Your Solar Return Chart

At this point, you know who your co-creator planet is, and you've gotten to know it in your birth chart. You understand what's hot or turned on in your birth chart and what that might mean for the events and quality of the year ahead. You've probably also figured out by now that multiple years of your life will be guided by the same planet. So what makes one different from the next? For example, you'll have many Venus-ruled years throughout your life, but they won't all be the same. They may echo or whisper to one another, but they won't be identical. What makes one Venus year different from another Venus year? Your solar return chart.

Your solar return chart is essentially the chart for your most recent birthday. More precisely, it's the chart for the moment the Sun returns to the same spot in the zodiac it was in at your birth, which may technically be a little bit before or after your actual birthday this year. For example, if your Sun was at 6 degrees and 18 minutes of Scorpio when you were born, the moment the real-time Sun reaches 6 degrees and 18 minutes of Scorpio marks the moment of your solar return.

Your solar return chart gives you even more information about how the year may feel and what potential you can squeeze out of it. It can identify additional focal points of the year, whether there will be any distractions or tangents, and what those might be. It can also give you insight into how powerful and willing your co-creator planet is this year. Going back to our Venus example, there will be Venus years when Venus is very happy and powerful in the solar return and years when Venus may be struggling to do its thing and be itself.

The co-creator's happiness or condition in the solar return chart reflects the capacity it has to deliver for you this year. If it's stronger than your natal co-creator, fantastic! You can expect a bit more juice to come your way. If it's about equal to your natal co-creator, things will unfold as usual with their regular speed and characteristics. And if your solar return co-creator is less happy or less powerful than your natal co-creator, it may not have a lot to offer, and you may subjectively experience the year as full of delays, obstacles, and distractions or just going in a different way than you imagined.

To follow along in this chapter, you're going to need a special copy of your solar return chart. I recommend getting what's called a bi-wheel, which shows your natal chart in the center and your current solar return chart on the outside. When calculating your solar return chart, be sure to set the location as your place of birth and use whole-sign houses. Check the "Resources" section in the back of the book for a link to an online calculator that will create a bi-wheel for you. I also recommend turning off any extra bells and whistles like asteroids and even aspect lines so that you have a clean and clear chart.

The natal chart is the root of everything in astrology. So, it's really important to evaluate your solar return chart within the context of your natal chart. The solar return chart should rarely, if ever, be read independently. The natal chart is where everything begins. It's the chart that describes your life's potential. The solar return chart simply helps you figure out to what degree that potential is fulfilled. The solar return chart doesn't have any potential on its own.

You can go as in-depth as you like when assessing your solar return chart, but I like to keep it to the essentials. You've already gathered so much information from your natal chart, and it's important to have a cap or astrology begins to get overwhelming and unhelpful. There are basically three things I look at in a solar return chart. I'll list them here and then go into each in depth:

1. Your co-creator in the solar return chart: Where is it and how powerful is it? What does it have to offer?
2. The ascendant of the solar return chart and how it interacts with your natal chart: Where does it fall in your natal chart and what does it activate?
3. Any aspects between your solar return chart and your natal chart that involve your co-creator.

Anything beyond this is just extra or icing on the cake. When I'm reading charts for clients, it's rare for me to go beyond these three things, and I encourage you to cap it here too.

• • • • • • •

Step 1: Evaluate Your Solar Return Co-Creator

Good news! You already know how to evaluate a planet using the CLEAR method. To assess your solar return co-creator, you're simply going to repeat those same steps. You can flip back to chapter 3 for the detailed instructions, but we'll also do an example together here.

In our example chart, Angela is advancing into a third-house year. There are no planets in her natal third house, so its planetary ruler will act as a co-creator. The zodiac sign of Libra is in the third house, making Venus the co-creator for the year. Angela's first step would be to evaluate her natal Venus using the CLEAR method and prompts from chapter 3. Let's pretend that's complete, and now she's going to repeat that process for her solar return Venus.

C: Club

First, we want to know if solar return Venus belongs to the club, or sect, of the chart. If we draw a line from the solar return ascendant to the solar return descendant to create the horizon, we notice that the Sun is above the horizon, making this solar return a day chart. Venus is a night-club planet and therefore does not belong to the club in charge. This isn't terrible; it just means that Venus may be asked to do some things that are outside of its comfort zone this year.

The other club that Venus belongs to is the benefic club. This is positive! Benefic planets are life-affirming. Their actions are to grow, expand, reward, connect, honor, and begin.

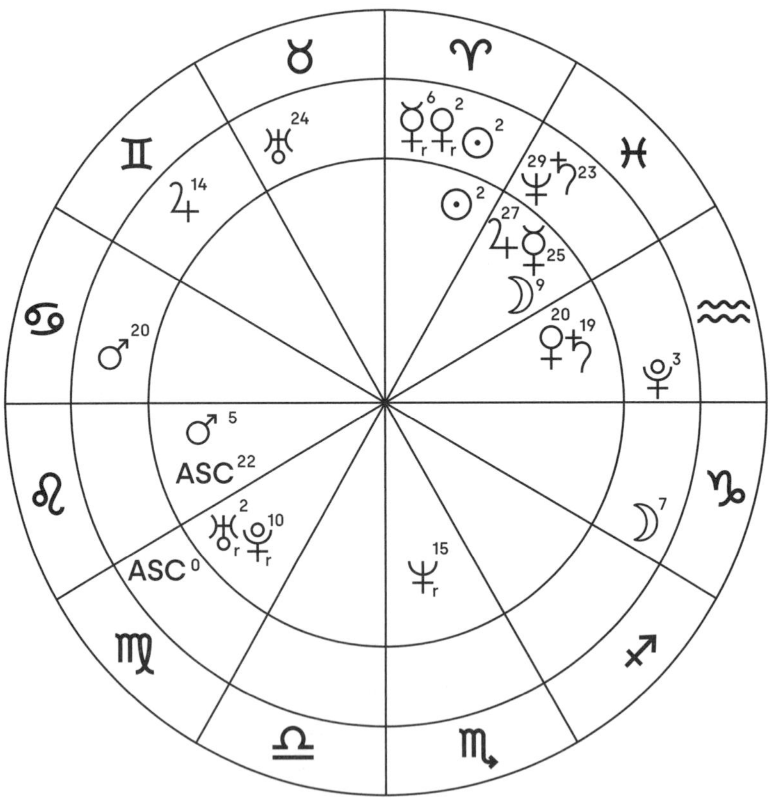

Bi-wheel chart. Angela's natal chart is in the inner circle, and her solar return chart is in the outer circle.

L: Location

Now we want to evaluate the zodiac sign and house location of solar return Venus. The solar return Venus is in the sign of Aries. Aries is a Fire sign, meaning that it's masculine or yang in expression. This Venus will behave in a more extroverted, active, and fast way. Aries is also a cardinal sign, meaning this version of Venus is likely to be more forceful and direct than other versions. However, there's one more important detail here. Venus meets our criteria for being in an "extreme" condition. Aries is one of the signs of Venus's detriment. This is a zodiacal environment that's extremely foreign to Venus. Aries belongs to Mars, and if we imagined it as a home, it would be filled with power tools and blowtorches and sharp knives. Venus just wants to love and connect—what's it going to do with a blowtorch?! In order to get its desires accomplished, Venus will have to be extra creative in this unideal environment. A solar return co-creator in detriment may feel unstable or need extra time or outside help to do its thing.

What about the house position? Remember, you're always evaluating the solar return chart in the context of the natal chart. What *natal* house does the solar return Venus fall in? In Angela's case, it's the ninth house. This solar return Venus will be using ninth-house topics like spirituality, wisdom, higher education, and publishing to do its work this year. We also know that the ninth house is cadent, meaning that Venus is on a slippery slope and although it may be very good at managing spiritual matters, it doesn't have a ton of practical footing or support. However, it could be much worse. Even though it's somewhat weak, the ninth house is still considered favorable because it aspects the ascendant.

E: Energy

Remember, energy refers to a planet's speed and direction. If you take a closer look at this solar return Venus, you'll notice a tiny *r* next to it. That indicates that this Venus is actually retrograde. This means it's moving very slowly and is likely to do its work at a more leisurely pace and may face a few delays or tangents.

A: Appearance

A planet's visibility can also affect its performance. Remember, visibility hinges on a planet's proximity to the Sun. From chapter 3, you know that when a planet is within 15 degrees of the Sun, it's invisible. In Angela's solar return chart, the Sun and Venus are both at 2 degrees of Aries. This certainly meets the criteria for invisible. This makes the solar return Venus more likely to do its work in private and less likely to put things on display. It may feel more comfortable working behind the scenes instead of being the front-runner.

R: Relationships

And finally, it's time to evaluate the relationships or aspects solar return Venus makes with other solar return planets. Remember, to keep things streamlined, we're focusing on whole-sign aspects and not worrying about degrees. First, check for conjunctions or copresence. Solar return Venus makes two conjunctions, one with the solar return Sun and one with solar return Mercury retrograde. Now, look across the wheel to Libra and check for an opposition. Nothing there. Next, check if solar return Venus makes any squares. The signs that square Aries are Capricorn and Cancer. In this solar return chart, Venus receives a square from the Moon in Capricorn (helpful), but it also receives a square from Mars in Cancer—that could create a little friction. Trines are up next. Look to the other Fire signs (Leo and Sagittarius) to see if Venus receives a trine. Nothing there. And finally, the sextile. Aries makes a sextile with the signs of Aquarius and Gemini. In the solar return chart, Venus's friend Jupiter is hanging out in Gemini. We love this. It might offset a bit of the tension Mars is adding. And although we aren't paying too much attention to outer planets in this step, it's worth noting that Pluto is also making a sextile with Venus.

Step 2: Compare and Contrast Your Co-Creators

Okay, great work! Hopefully you're getting the hang of the CLEAR method by now. The next step is to compare and contrast your natal co-creator with your solar return co-creator. This will tell you more about the quality of your year ahead. To start, I find it helpful to write out a little two-column list where you compare the two side-by-side. For example, here's a side-by-side comparison of Angela's natal Venus and solar return Venus.

	Natal Venus	Solar Return Venus
Club	Belongs	Does not belong
Location	Aquarius, 7th house (angular, favorable)	Aries (detriment), 9th house (cadent, favorable)
Energy	Fast, direct	Slow, retrograde
Appearance	Visible	Invisible
Relationships	Conjunction: Saturn (malefic) Opposition: Mars (malefic) Sextile: Sun	Conjunction: Sun and Mercury Square: Moon and Mars (malefic) Sextile: Jupiter (benefic) and Pluto

Now comes the hard part. Which co-creator is strongest? This assessment may feel very subjective at first and that's okay. The judgment part of astrology is quite hard (it's why professionals exist!), and I encourage you to go with your gut instinct.

In Angela's case, I think natal Venus is stronger than solar return Venus. Does this mean the year will be terrible? No! But it does mean that Angela will likely need to be flexible with her plans and perhaps ask for outside support when it comes to Venus topics, which for her are career (tenth house) and communication (third house). Venus may not grant Angela the biggest career success of her life this year, but it will bring an opportunity to do tenth- and third-house things in a way she never has before. Solar return Venus operates in a very unique and against-the-grain way compared to natal Venus. It's likely that Angela will decide to make some professional changes, which may make her feel a little unstable or out of her depth for a while, but it's completely workable. She might decide to get some outside assistance, like coaching, in order to make career decisions this year.

Step 3: Evaluate Your Solar Return Ascendant

If you still have some brain space, there's another place you can look for extra information about the year—the solar return ascendant. Find this degree in your natal chart and notice what natal house it's located in and if it is conjunct any natal planets. Just like you identified themes with profections, the solar return ascendant and where it falls in your natal chart also identifies threads and storylines that may be woven into your year.

In Angela's case, the solar return ascendant is at zero degrees of Virgo, which falls in her natal second house. This means that personal finance, spending and saving habits, and livelihood will be highlighted for her this year as well. It's also very close to her natal Uranus, the planet of innovation and reversals, which reemphasizes the themes we've already seen about taking an alternative path or making some changes.

Step 4: Identify Your Solar Return Transits

You know by now that a transit occurs when a real-time planet in today's sky interacts with a planet in your birth chart. You also know that transits can become overwhelming without a prioritization system. Are you ready to simplify them even more? Let's do it.

From an ancient astrology perspective, the relationships (a.k.a. aspects) between your solar return planets and your natal planets act as the transits for your entire year. For example, Angela's solar return Venus is making a trine to her natal Mars. That's a "transit" that's active for the entire year, not just the day of her solar return. Instead of watching the many transits changing day-to-day, you might choose to simply use the solar return chart as a snapshot of what celestial weather will be influencing you for the next twelve months.

Let's be honest, looking at a bi-wheel chart and picking out the aspects is hard work if you're not a professional astrologer. So for this section, I suggest using software that'll spit out an aspect list for you. The free site I reference in the "Resources" section will not only give you a bi-wheel chart, it'll list the aspects between the two charts. What I go through here is how to take that list and whittle it down. If you're an astrology nerd and want to do this by hand, I suggest only picking out the aspects that have an orb of 3 degrees or less.

Here's Angela's list of transits for the year. The solar return planet is listed first, and the natal planet is listed second.

Moon sextile Moon

Mercury trine Mars

Venus conjunct the Sun

Venus trine Mars

Saturn conjunct Mercury

Uranus sextile Mercury

Uranus square Venus

Uranus sextile Jupiter

Uranus square the Ascendant

Neptune conjunct Jupiter

Pluto sextile the Sun

Pluto opposite Mars

Whew, that's a lot! But here's the thing: Most of them don't matter. Yes, I said that. Having a list this long makes astrology dizzying and mind-boggling. What we need to do next is identify the most pivotal planetary relationships that Angela will actually feel and notice this year. Here's the cheat sheet:

Aspects involving the co-creator

Conjunctions between solar return planets and natal planets

Transits through the sign/house of the year

Remember that Angela's co-creator is Venus, so our first step is to pick out anything on the list that includes Venus. We could stop here and that would be sufficient. But because I know you love astrology, let's keep going. In my opinion, conjunctions from solar return planets to natal planets are vital and will be very obvious in how they express. They really activate the natal planet and wake it up. And finally, we want to check the sign/house of the year for any planets. Angela's sign of the year is Libra, and it's free and clear of any planets.

Finished. We've cut our list in half! Check it out:

Uranus square Venus

Venus conjunct the Sun

Venus trine Mars

Saturn conjunct Mercury

Neptune conjunct Jupiter

Could we make a case for other aspects to make the list? Of course! Although I'm doing my best to systematize this, the process for an actual astrologer can be a bit more extensive and subjective. All that said, if there's something on the original list that's really speaking to you, trust your intuition. But in my opinion, less is more.

So now what? Now you can read about these transits in their corresponding planet chapter. For example, to understand what Uranus square Venus means, head to the Venus chapter. To get insight on Neptune conjunct Jupiter, head to the Jupiter chapter.

• • • • • • •

Sovereign Astrology Mindset Moment

I'm just going to tell you right now: There will be a solar return chart in your future that you don't like. It won't look "good" astrologically, and it will be really tempting to go into catastrophe mode and think the worst. My challenge for you is to find the good stuff. Be creative. Spin the narrative. What beauty can come from this chart? Who can this chart serve? What can this chart make? Instead of thinking, *What's going to happen to me?* think, *How am I going to happen to it? What am I going to do with it?*

Nice work! That was *so* much astrology. Take a break, let all the pieces settle and simmer, and then work through the reflection questions below.

• • • • • • •

Reflection Questions

Now that you have all the astrological facts about your solar return chart, it's time to check in with your inner knowing. Invite your solar return co-creator and your natal co-creator to write with you.

Which of your co-creators is strongest?

How are they similar?

How are they different?

What new approaches, opportunities, or challenges does your solar return co-creator offer your natal co-creator?

Now that you know this, how can you adjust your mindset and your plans?

With your solar return in mind, what reminders, words, and intentions do you have for your year?

fifteen

Keep the Magic Going

Take a moment to recognize how much astrology you've just learned. (So much!) You know how to identify your co-creator planet and interpret its potential in your natal chart. You know how to compare and contrast your co-creator planet with its solar return counterpart and make a judgment about how it affects your year ahead. You know how to connect with your co-creator planet through prayer, journaling, and practical to-dos. And you know how to navigate astrology fear if it ever pops up. In these final pages, I want to leave you with some tips and practices to help you keep the magic of profections going all year long.

Going Deeper: Monthly Profections

If you've fallen in love with annual profections like I have, you'll be excited to know that you can do even more with them. Cue monthly profections. Each month of your year is linked to a particular house and therefore a particular co-creator planet too. Monthly profections operate just like annual profections but faster.

Here's how it works. You start your first month in the house of the year. For example, let's pretend your birthday is September 17, and you're in a fifth-house year. The first month (beginning on your birthday) is linked to the fifth house. One month later on October 17, you advance into the sixth house, and one month after that on November 17, you advance into the seventh house, and so on (see below).

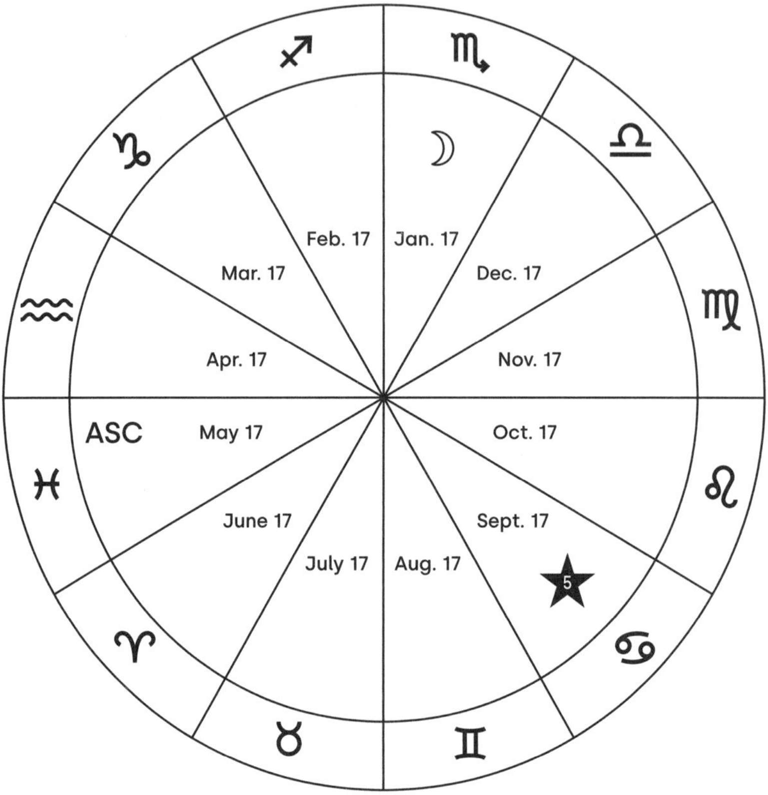

Monthly profections. Start from the house of the year.

September 17: Fifth house (birthday)

October 17: Sixth house

November 17: Seventh house

December 17: Eighth house

January 17: Ninth house

February 17: Tenth house

March 17: Eleventh house

April 17: Twelfth house

May 17: First house

June 17: Second house

July 17: Third house

August 17: Fourth house

Just like in annual profections, when a house is highlighted by monthly profections, everything in that house and the co-creator planet either located in or ruling that house gets switched on. If you want a crash course on how your chart works, follow monthly profections closely. It's a speedy way to learn how each planet in your natal chart behaves and what types of topics and events it brings about. In a way, you live your whole life in a year. Pretty wild, right?!

Something to pay close attention to in monthly profections is when you advance into the house that contains your co-creator. In our fifth-house example, let's pretend Cancer is in the fifth house. There aren't any planets in this house, so that means the Moon (the ruler of Cancer) is the co-creator. In this example chart, the Moon is located in the ninth house. That means when the monthly profection comes to the ninth house, we have a super activation. In our example, that would be the month beginning on January 17. When the monthly profection comes to the house containing your co-creator, you may notice more pivotal events or storylines of the year unfold.

Weekly Co-Creator Ritual

I find it really nourishing to connect with my co-creator planet as regularly as possible, and I encourage you to do the same. It's one thing to identify your co-creator planet once and then promptly forget about it. It's a totally different (and much more powerful) thing to keep connecting with your co-creator all year round. I want you to think of this as a real relationship—one that evolves and deepens over time. Just like human relationships, it can be hard to find the time to get together. Luckily, astrology has a lot of fun ways to schedule things, whether they be practical work tasks or spiritual practices like planet channeling. An easy way to remember it's time to connect with your co-creator is to schedule a recurring get-together on its day of the week. Yes, each planet rules a certain day. These are called the planetary days. For example, if your co-creator is Jupiter, you'll block off some time each Thursday to connect with it. I've listed all the planetary days below:

Monday: Moon

Tuesday: Mars

Wednesday: Mercury

Thursday: Jupiter

Friday: Venus

Saturday: Saturn

Sunday: Sun

So, it's scheduled. Now, what do you do? The first thing I like to do is check where my co-creator planet is in the sky right now. If your co-creator is a slow planet like Saturn, it may not have moved very far, but if it's a fast planet like Mercury, it may have completely changed zodiac signs since you last checked in. After dating your page (astrologers always date their pages!), write the current zodiac location and maybe even the degree of your co-creator planet at the top. I consider this essential information. Remember, when your co-creator planet shifts signs, changes directions, or is involved in a major aspect, your life changes in quality and direction too. If you have time, you could even do a quick internet search and read a few articles on that placement to get some ideas about what it might mean for you.

I think it's also great to remember your intentions for the year during your weekly check-in. If you did the birthday ritual in the previous chapter, take a minute to reread your answers to the reflection questions, especially the last one: What reminders, words, and intentions do you have for your year? This is also a perfect time to reread any answers to the reflection questions from your co-creator's respective chapter.

Now that you've gathered the celestial facts and taken a moment to remember, it's time to connect. As you know from the planet channeling section, I like to write a very casual greeting as a way to call in my co-creator. Remember, you're connecting with a friend and a supportive presence. It might be as simple as *Hi, Jupiter. Thanks for taking time out of your day to meet with me.*

From here, you can really do whatever calls to you. I'm a big fan of personal authority, and I encourage you to create your own ritual. But for the sake of example, here are a few ideas on how to foster a rich cosmic conversation.

• • • • • • •

Start with gratitude. Take a few minutes to write a couple of lines of thanks to your co-creator planet. Thank it for working on your behalf (even if you can't see what it's doing just yet!) and praise it for any major events or opportunities that it's brought about. It might go something like this:

Jupiter, I just want to express how grateful I am that you're taking care of my life behind the scenes. I confess I don't fully understand what you're doing just yet, but I trust you. Thank you for guiding me and having my best interests at heart.

Then, allow your co-creator planet to express gratitude for you. Yes, really. Just like a real friend would probably repay a compliment, let your co-creator planet shower you with some encouragement. For example:

Aw, thanks, Claire. I appreciate you too. I want you to know that I see you stretching yourself and stepping out of your comfort zone. I know I've asked you to do a lot lately, and I just want you to know that I have your back.

Now, ask your co-creator the following questions and freely write the answers until you feel complete:

Co-creator, what's one thing you want me to remember this week?

Co-creator, how can I support you this week?

Finally, end by telling your co-creator how it can support you. Give it an assignment. Remember, your co-creator planet loves to do good work for you, but it needs instruction. This is your opportunity to do that. It might look something like this:

Jupiter, I'd really appreciate it if you'd help me write the conclusion to my book this week. Please bring me fresh ideas and concrete direction. Thank you!

And that's that. This is a simple way to keep in contact with your co-creator all year long. Keeping up with your co-creator is like reviewing your goals and plans regularly—it means more significant life shifts and more intentional change. If you feel inspired, make a dedicated co-creator journal where you can keep these check-ins all in one place and reread them throughout the year.

Acknowledgments

I'm beyond grateful to have had the opportunity to write a second book. Writing is my dream, and there are so many people who make it possible. First in line, of course, is my husband, Ryan. Thank you for your never-ending support and your unwavering belief that I can do this. I love you. Thank you to my entire family for supporting and loving me no matter what weird path I choose to go down. I love that I can be myself with you. To my friends, Stephanie Keiko Kong, Miranda Braithwaite, and everyone in the astropreneur social community, thank you for checking on me throughout the process—our chats give me life.

Thank you to the many people I interviewed for this book. Whether your story made it to the page or not, you were invaluable to the process. Thank you for your vulnerability and willingness to share your life with me. It was my honor and delight to listen! Special thanks to Angela for allowing me to use her chart as an example. (You're my favorite!)

Thank you to Jacqueline Fisch and The Intuitive Writing School for holding space for me as I completed the first draft. Thank you for teaching me that writing doesn't have to be lonely!

Thank you, Shambhala, for giving me the opportunity to do what I love again. I want to especially thank Beth Frankl for seeking me out. This project was an instant, full-body yes! Much love and appreciation to my editors, Beth Frankl and Dianna Able.

Thanks also to the entire Shambhala team: copyeditor Jill Rogers, proofreader Sandra Korinchak, cover art director Daniel Urban-Brown, cover designer Meredith Jarrett, and the M+P team of Mir Murphy and Abigail LeFleur-Shaffer.

Finally, I want to express my deepest respect and gratitude to all of my astrological teachers, especially those who taught me the techniques featured in this book. To the luminaries of astrology, my greatest thanks: Demetra George, Kelly Surtees, Chris Brennan, and let's not forget Vettius Valens.

Appendix

Glyph Key

Zodiac Signs	Glyph	Planets and Points	Glyph
Aries	♈	Ascendant	ASC
Taurus	♉	Sun	☉
Gemini	♊	Moon	☽
Cancer	♋	Mercury	☿
Leo	♌	Venus	♀
Virgo	♍	Mars	♂
Libra	♎	Jupiter	♃
Scorpio	♏	Saturn	♄
Sagittarius	♐	Uranus	♅
Capricorn	♑	Neptune	♆
Aquarius	♒	Pluto	♇
Pisces	♓		

Resources

Planetary Attunements

For audio versions of all planetary attunements and the DIY Profection Project templates, head to www.astrologywithclaire.com /cosmicyear.

Where to Get Your Birth Chart

There are so many great options these days for calculating your birth chart, but my favorites are below. For the purposes of this book, I highly recommend using whole-sign houses, which you can toggle on in the settings.

Astro-Seek.com

Astro.com

Transit Tools

Honeycomb Collective Personal Astrological Almanac (https:// honeycomb.co)

Astro-Seek Personal Transit Calendar (https://horoscopes.astro -seek.com/personal-transit-calendar-monthly-astrology-transits)

Solar Return Bi-Wheel Calculator

Remember to set the location of your solar return chart as your birth location.

Astro-Seek (https://horoscopes.astro-seek.com/solar-return-chart)

Professional Software

If you're ready to take your astrology journey a step further, investing in professional software will allow you to calculate transits, solar return charts, and profections with ease.

Astro Gold (https://astrogold.io)

Solar Fire (https://alabe.com/solarfireV9.html)

Bibliography

Avelar, Helena, and Ribeiro, Luis. *On the Heavenly Spheres: A Treatise on Traditional Astrology*. Tempe, AZ: American Federation of Astrologers, Inc., 2010.

Avelar, Helena, and Ribeiro, Luis. *Traditional Astrology Course: Essential Concepts and Interpretation Basics*. Prisma Edições, 2019.

Brennan, Chris. *Annual Profections Timing Technique* (class). The Astrology School, 2015. https://courses.theastrologyschool.com/courses/annual-profections-timing-technique-class.

George, Demetra. *Ancient Astrology in Theory and Practice: A Manual of Traditional Techniques*. Vol. 1, *Assessing Planetary Condition*. Rubedo Press, 2019.

George, Demetra. *Ancient Astrology in Theory and Practice: A Manual of Traditional Techniques*. Vol. 2, *Delineating Planetary Meaning*. Rubedo Press, 2022.

George, Demetra. *Hellenistic Astrology 301: Time Lords* (certificate program). Demetra George (website). 2025. https://demetra-george.com/product/hellenistic-astrology-time-lords/.

Hand, Robert. *Planets in Transit: Life Cycles for Living*. Whitford Press, 1976.

Ma'shar, Abu. *On Solar Revolutions*. Translated and edited by Benjamin N. Dykes. The Cazimi Press, 2010.

Surtees, Kelly. *Profections and Solar Returns for Better Annual Forecasting* (webinar). Kelly's Astrology, 2019. https://www.kellysastrology.com/product/profections/.

Usher, Joy. *A Tiny Universe's Companion: Popular Techniques in Traditional Astrology*. Xlibris, 2018.

Valens, Vettius. *The Anthology*. Translated by Mark T. Riley. Amor Fati Publications, 2022.

About the Author

Claire Gallagher has been a professional astrologer for over a decade. With a focus on presence before prediction, Claire uses astrology to help people feel better today instead of future-tripping about tomorrow. Whether she's doing a reading, moving with the Moon, or teaching planetary journaling, Claire's mission is to help others hear and follow their inner wisdom. You can find her at www.astrologywithclaire.com.